THE ROYAL LOVER'S GUIDE TO
LONDON

THE ROYAL LOVER'S GUIDE TO
LONDON

ANGELA YOUNGMAN

WHITE OWL

AN IMPRINT OF PEN & SWORD BOOKS LTD.
YORKSHIRE – PHILADELPHIA

First published in Great Britain in 2023 by
White Owl
An imprint of
Pen & Sword Books Ltd
Yorkshire - Philadelphia

Copyright © Angela Youngman, 2023

ISBN 978 1 39900 170 0

The right of Angela Youngman to be identified as author of
this work has been asserted by her in accordance with the
Copyright, Designs and Patents Act 1988.

A CIP catalogue record for this book is available from the
British Library.

Printed and bound by Short Run Press Limited, Exeter.
Design: SJmagic DESIGN SERVICES, India.

Pen & Sword Books Ltd incorporates the imprints of Pen
& Sword Books Archaeology, Atlas, Aviation, Battleground,
Discovery, Family History, History, Maritime, Military, Naval,
Politics, Railways, Select, Transport, True Crime, Fiction,
Frontline Books, Leo Cooper, Praetorian Press, Seaforth
Publishing, Wharncliffe and White Owl.

For a complete list of Pen & Sword titles please contact

PEN & SWORD BOOKS LIMITED
47 Church Street, Barnsley, South Yorkshire, S70 2AS, England
E-mail: enquiries@pen-and-sword.co.uk
Website: www.pen-and-sword.co.uk

or

PEN AND SWORD BOOKS
1950 Lawrence Rd, Havertown, PA 19083, USA
E-mail: Uspen-and-sword@casematepublishers.com
Website: www.penandswordbooks.com

CONTENTS

PICTURE ACKNOWLEDGEMENTS

With thanks to

All England Lawn Tennis Museum
Arsenal
Bank of England
Chelsea Physic Garden
Claridges
Dulwich Picture Gallery
Floris
Fortnums
Harrods
Harvey Nichols
House of Garrard
Imperial War Museum
Karis Youngman
Kia Oval
London Zoo
Madame Tussauds
Old Royal Naval College
Partridges
Paxton & Whitfield
Prestat
RAF Hendon
Regent Street.
Sadlers Wells Theatre
Science Museum
Stanley Gibbons
The 02 Arena
Twinings
Wiltons

INTRODUCTION

London and the Royal Family are inextricably intertwined. Generations of monarchs have been crowned, married and buried within its environs. Their lives have centred around London and it has been the scene of many dramatic events that have determined the fate of the country, including treason, rebellions, riots and architecture. The British royal family is one of the oldest in the world, tracing back through various royal lines to the Saxon kings.

For over a thousand years, William the Conqueror's White Tower has dominated London, while Queen Victoria presided over dramatic change in the fabric of the city due to the coming of the railways. Her consort, Prince Albert, instigated the creation of a museum quarter in Kensington and a Great Exhibition in Hyde Park, as well as numerous bridges over the Thames. The young King Richard II faced Wat Tyler's peasant rebellion at Smithfield, and Richard III may or may not have murdered the Princes in the Tower of London. The policies of Henry VIII led to the closure of the monasteries that had played such an important role in London for centuries, as well as enabling him to gain ownership of the spectacular Hampton Court Palace. The activities of Charles I in Westminster resulted in a civil war, while his sons Charles II and James helped Londoners fight the Great Fire of London.

London has witnessed numerous royal love affairs. In 1290, Edward I mourned the death of his beloved wife, Eleanor of Castile, by installing memorial crosses at all the points her coffin rested between Nottingham and London, where she was buried in Westminster Abbey. The final cross in Westminster was destroyed during the Civil War, and later replaced with a statue of Charles I. In the 1860s, the Victorians set out to recreate that final Eleanor Cross, installing an elaborate monument just outside Charing Cross Station.

Henry VIII's romantic entanglements were played out within his premier palaces of Whitehall, Tower of London, Greenwich, Richmond and Hampton Court. It was a story which had a massive impact, resulting in a major change of religious and foreign policy that dominated royal and state affairs for centuries. In total contrast, George IV hated his wife so much he refused to let her be crowned Queen.

Not far from Charing Cross is Covent Garden, where Charles II enjoyed many hours in the company of his beloved mistress, Nell Gwynne. The love match between Victoria and Albert helped transform the architectural fabric of London. Prince Albert's name is immortalised across London, from the Albert Bridge to the Albert Hall, and from the Albert Embankment to the Royal Albert Dock.

London is where the first public knowledge of the relationship between Princess Elizabeth (later Queen Elizabeth II) and Prince Philip emerged, and saw the deepening relationships between Prince William and Kate Middleton, Prince Harry and Meghan Markle, and Princess Eugenie and Jack Brooksbank develop into marriage. In 2022 it was the setting for the poignant funeral of Queen Elizabeth II attracting global attention and in 2023, the location for the coronation of her successor King Charles III formerly Prince of Wales at Westminster Abbey.

Thousands of people come every year to see the stunning places associated with the Royal Family, to watch spectacular ceremonies like Changing of the Guard or simply to explore the history and heritage of Royal London. It is a city that plays a key role in major royal events such as Queen Elizabeth II's Diamond, Gold and Platinum Jubilees, the Coronation, State Opening of Parliament, the Royal Wedding of the heir to the throne as well as Queen Elizabeth II's own marriage to Prince Philip and is where the senior members of the Royal

Family lead the nation in mourning on Remembrance Day, State visits and national celebrations.

Browsing through this book will enable you to find the all the locations linked to royalty. Discover where the royals shop, the London companies who supply the royal households and even the railway stations that they use when travelling by train.

KEY MEMBERS OF THE ROYAL FAMILY October 2022

King Charles III (formerly Prince of Wales and eldest son of Queen Elizabeth & Prince Philip, Duke of Edinburgh)

The Queen Consort Camilla, former Duchess of Cornwall

The Prince of Wales William, Duke of Cornwall and Duke of Cambridge

The Princess of Wales Catherine, Duchess of Cornwall, Duchess of Cambridge and before her marriage was known as Kate Middleton

Princess Anne The Princess Royal (daughter of Queen Elizabeth & Prince Philip)

Prince Edward and his wife Sophie, Earl and Countess of Wessex (son of Queen Elizabeth & Prince Philip)

1

THE ROYAL RIVER

The River Thames has always been a royal river, linking royal residences between Hampton Court and Greenwich. Monarchs, princes and princesses have made their homes along the river or close by. For centuries, it was an incredibly busy river, providing the quickest and most reliable method of transport. Hundreds of boats passed along the river every day, as well as crossing backwards and forwards from one bank to the other. The Pool of London was the most crowded port in the world, and it is said that people could almost walk along the line of boats moored in the Thames. Getting a boat ride across the river was faster than walking across London Bridge.

It has always been a celebratory route for royal processions as well as providing rapid access for prisoners being sent to the Tower of London – as Queen Anne Boleyn, Queen Katherine Howard and the young Princess Elizabeth (later Elizabeth I) discovered. King Henry VIII owned two royal barges known as the *Lyon* and the *Greyhound* while the eighteenth century royal barge of Prince Frederick can now be

Seen from the air, London's West End with the River Thames in the distance.

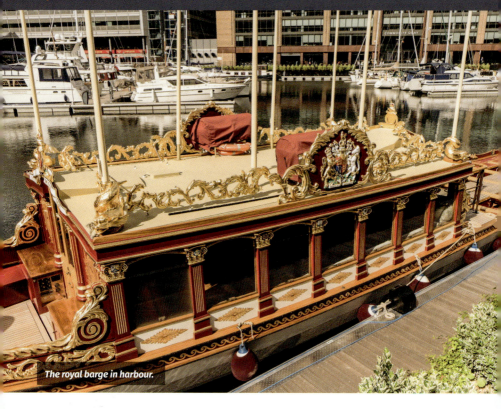

The royal barge in harbour.

seen at the National Maritime Museum, Greenwich.

Official Royal Watermen were responsible for providing royal waterborne transport – a service that was still used extensively until the mid-nineteenth century. Today it is mainly ceremonial, with just twenty-four Queen's Watermen receiving a token salary of just £3.50! They were last seen in action on the water in the stunning river procession that formed the climax of Queen Elizabeth's Diamond Jubilee celebrations in 2012. Thousands of people lined the banks to watch, while

millions more across the globe watched on screen.

Queen Elizabeth travelled on board a Thames barge known as the *Spirit of Chartwell* accompanied by the Prince of Wales (now King Charles III) and Duchess of Cornwall, the Duke and Duchess of Cambridge and Prince Harry. The Duke of York and his daughters Princesses Beatrice and Eugenie, along with the Earl and Countess of Wessex, travelled immediately behind on the *Havengore*.

Starting at Cadogan Pier, Wandsworth, the flotilla of over

1,000 vessels led by the Queen's barge travelled under fourteen of London's bridges: Chelsea Bridge, Grosvenor Bridge, Vauxhall Bridge, Lambeth Bridge, Westminster Bridge, Hungerford Bridge, Golden Jubilee Bridge, Waterloo Bridge, Blackfriars Bridge, Blackfriars Railway Bridge, Millennium Bridge, Southwark Bridge, Cannon Street Railway Bridge, London Bridge and Tower Bridge.

This was not the first time that Queen Elizabeth II had participated in such a procession – although it was by far the largest of all her river pageants.

Six weeks after her coronation in 1953, Queen Elizabeth took part in a Royal River Pageant organised by the Lord Mayor of London. On that occasion just 150 vessels took part, with the Queen travelling on board *Nore*, the Port of London Authority's inspection launch. A further pageant was held in 1977 in honour of Queen Elizabeth's Silver Jubilee when 140 vessels were involved. Queen Elizabeth again travelled in another Port of London vessel, also named *Nore*. The 2002 Golden Jubilee was marked by a tribute event, coinciding with the Thames Festival.

HMS Belfast *framed against Tower Bridge on the River Thames.*

Other Royal river links include the opening of the new London Bridge by Queen Elizabeth in 1973, the opening of the Thames Barrier in 1984, and in 2002 the opening of the Millennium Footbridge. In 1994 the Royal Yacht *Britannia* rode upstream to moor beside HMS *Belfast*, and in 2000 Queen Elizabeth continued the long royal tradition of travelling along the Thames using waterborne transport to launch the Millennium celebrations at the Millennium Dome, Greenwich.

Every year, the Company of Watermen hold their own unique race along the Thames. The Doggetts Coat and Badge Race involves members of the Watermen's guild rowing at speed between London Bridge and Cadogan Pier Chelsea.

Hampton Court Palace

East Molesey, KT8 9AU

Impressively dramatic, Hampton Court Palace is one of the most stunning of all the Royal Palaces. Built by Thomas Wolsey in the sixteenth century as a palace fit for a king, it quickly became exactly that when Henry VIII took over the building and extended it, making it the centre of Tudor court life. All his wives stayed at Hampton Court – and there are stories that the ghost of the unfortunate Katherine Howard runs screaming through a gallery. In the seventeenth century, William III and Mary II ordered an additional building to be created by Sir Christopher Wren.

Hampton Court Palace has continued to attract attention from modern royals. There was a bomb scare just before the arrival of the Prince and Princess of Wales in 1986 for *The Times* 200th Anniversary Gala. The annual RHS Hampton Court Flower Show has led to regular royal visits, while in 2016 the Duchess of Cambridge opened the popular Tudor-inspired Magic Garden for children. Since then, she has shown off a version of the RHS Back to Nature garden that she helped design in 2019 for the Chelsea Flower Show. Other royal visits include the launch of a Royal School of Needlework exhibition by Queen Consort Camilla and concerts in aid of the Sentabale charity attended by Prince Harry. It is a favourite venue for royal events – sometimes controversial as this is where King Charles made his famous 'carbuncle' comments in 1984 referring to the style of a planned extension to the National Gallery. In 2022, Prince William, Prince of Wales attended the annual Tusk Conservations Awards at Hampton Court Palace.

Why not follow in royal footsteps by holding a wedding here? Various rooms such as the Little Banqueting House can be booked for weddings. Hampton Court was the venue for

The grand entrance to Hampton Court Palace in Richmond.

Henry VIII's wedding to Katherine Parr, as well as the honeymoon location for Charles II and his bride Catherine of Braganza, when boats in the shape of swans sailed around the Long Water in a romantic gesture.

Explore the unique Georgian Chocolate Kitchen or the Great Kitchens built for Henry VIII's court. Stroll through discreet courtyards, discover the private and state apartments used by Kings and Queens over the centuries and admire the sumptuous tapestries that bedeck the walls of the medieval Great Hall. Investigate the sixty acres of gardens, including a Capability Brown landscape. Special events are often held here, including a stunning Christmas ice rink.

Entry fees are payable.

Opening hours
Daily except 24 – 26 December:
  10am – 6pm

Nearest Train
Hampton Court, five minutes walk
  (trains run from London Waterloo
  every thirty minutes).
Or take the traditional royal route
  along the Thames – boats leave
  regularly from Hampton Court pier to
  Westminster Bridge.
www.hrp.org.uk/hampton-court-palace

2

KENSINGTON AND CHELSEA

Albert Memorial

Kensington Gardens, WC2 2UH

Commissioned by Queen Victoria in honour of her beloved Albert, who died of typhoid aged 41, the memorial was designed by Sir George Gilbert Scott and is extremely ornate, reflecting the Prince's varied interests. It shows him seated, holding a catalogue of the Great Exhibition held in Hyde Park in 1851 which he inspired and organised. Surrounding the Prince are marble figures at each corner, representing Europe, Asia, Africa and America, while figures immediately above represent

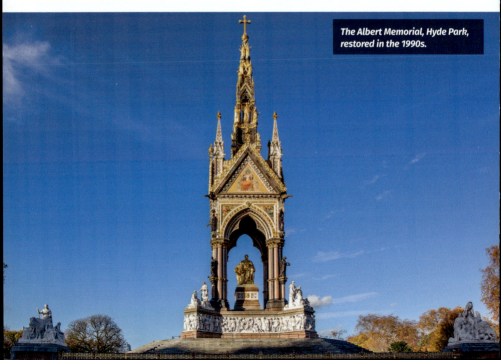

The Albert Memorial, Hyde Park, restored in the 1990s.

manufacture, commerce, agriculture and engineering. At the top of the monument are gilded bronze statues of angels and virtues, while at the base there is a frieze depicting 187 painters, poets, sculptors, musicians and architects. Princess Eugenie, a descendent of Queen Victoria and Prince Albert, highlighted the Albert Memorial as one of her iconic London attractions on her Instagram site.

Located directly opposite the Royal Albert Hall, the memorial was extensively restored in the 1990s, with more restoration undertaken in 2006. Guided tours are held on the first Sunday of each month, providing the opportunity to get much closer to the memorial than usual.

Garden opening hours
6am – 9pm daily

Nearest Underground
South Kensington 15 minutes
High Street Kensington 15 minutes

https://www.royalparks.org.uk/parks/
kensington-gardens/things-to-see-and-
do/memorials-fountains-and-statues/
the-albert-memorial

Bluebird Café

Kings Road, SW3 5UY

This has long been a popular dining venue for the Prince and Princess of Wales especially during their courtship. Kate was photographed here during the short breakup in her relationship with Prince William. Since then Kate and her sister Pippa Middleton have been seen dining on the terrace. The Bluebird Café describes itself as being 'a local neighbourhood restaurant on a grand scale'. There is a café and courtyard on the ground floor, plus a restaurant and bar on the first floor. In addition to the à la carte menu, the Bluebird is well known for weekend brunch and afternoon tea. Typical dishes include: fillet of sea bass; Jerusalem artichokes risotto; Bluebird Burger with cheese, bacon, onion and fries; boozy plums and vanilla ice cream.

Nearest Underground
South Kensington 5 minutes
Sloane Square 6 minutes

www.bluebirdcafe.co.uk

Bombay Brasserie

Courtfield Road, Kensington, SW7 4QH

This is Indian fine dining in style, combining Bengal, Gujerrat and Goa cooking styles with Mughal, Raj and even Portuguese influences, attracting a high-end audience. On one memorable evening Princess Diana showed up accompanied by Freddie Mercury, Kenny Everett and Cleo Rocos, and spent the evening drinking peach Bellinis. The Bombay Bar is still the perfect spot for a cocktail or glass of champagne, while the Brasserie offers a discreet, fashionable dining experience amid sumptuous décor. Typical dishes on offer include

Chicken Lababdar, Khumb Palak, Ajwaini Jhinga, Malai Kulfi and Cobra coffee.

Opening hours
12.30pm – 3pm and 7.30pm – 11.30pm daily

Nearest Underground
Gloucester Road 1 minute
South Kensington 8 minutes

www.bombayb.co.uk

Brook House Pub
68 New Kings Road, Fulham, SW6 4SG

A chic gastropub popular with trendsetters, the Brook House was where Prince Harry was seen relaxing with friends in January 2020, while negotiating stepping down as a senior royal.

The light and airy pub aims to be 'rustic, relaxed and welcoming to all' and has a calm green décor. It is combination of restaurant, pub and bar. Crab doughnuts and pork and apple sausages are among the typical dishes to be found on the menu.

Opening hours
Monday 5pm – 11pm
Tuesday to Wednesday 12 midday – 11pm
Thursday to Saturday 12 midday – 12 midnight
Sunday 12 midday – 10pm

Nearest Underground
Fulham Broadway 8 minutes
Parsons Green 10 minutes

www.brookhousefulham.com

Café Diana
Wellington Terrace, Bayswater, W2 4LW

Just outside the grounds of Kensington Gardens is an unusual little café dedicated to the memory of Diana, Princess of Wales. Opened in 1989, it has become an institution within the area. Café Diana 'celebrates the life of Princess Diana and is a tribute to all the good she did in life.' Apparently the Princess was known to drop into the café occasionally, and even brought Princes William and Harry in for cake. The owner comments on Facebook that 'the café, being situated opposite Kensington Gardens was named Café Diana as a homage to the nation's favourite Princess. We never expected the Princess to frequent our café and were absolutely delighted when she used to drop by. The café remains a spot for regulars, passers by and tourists alike.' Mementos of Diana can be found everywhere within the café, including a signed photograph and letters written by the Princess.

Café Diana sells a wide range of snack food, sandwiches, breakfast, salads, omelettes and fine coffee.

Opening hours
8am – 11pm

Nearest Underground
Notting Hill Gate 1 minute
Queensway 1 minute
Bayswater 3 minutes

www.cafediana.co.uk

Chelsea Physic Garden

66 Royal Hospital Road, Chelsea, SW3 4HS (public access via Swan Walk)

One of the oldest botanical gardens in the UK, it was established as the apothecaries' garden in 1673 by the Worshipful Society of Apothecaries and is a real gem. Renowned for his interest in gardening, it is no surprise that King Charles has been patron of the Chelsea Physic Garden since 2003. He visited in 2008, marking the 25th anniversary of the garden opening to the public, and warned of the need to protect medicinal plants from extinction and that studying plants was essential. The site now contains over 5,000 edible, useful and medicinal plants, many of which have changed the world. There are over 100 types of tree, including pomegranates, mulberries, grapefruit and the UK's largest fruiting olive tree. One hot summer, this provided 7lb of ripe olives. Stroll through the Victorian glasshouses and cool fernery, discover the oldest rock garden in Europe, dating back to 1773, and take a trip to the Canary Islands and Madeira to see a superb collection of native plants.

Entry fee

Opening hours
11am – 6pm daily

Nearest Underground
Sloane Square 13 minutes

www.chelseaphysicgarden.co.uk

Lush greenery at the Chelsea Physic Garden.

Chucs

226 Westbourne Grove, Notting Hill, W11 2RH

Meghan, Duchess of Sussex was spotted dining at Chucs in January 2019 with her newly appointed deputy communications secretary Christian Jones. An Italian restaurant, Chucs operates from four locations across London but Meghan opted for this one. The décor is a little unusual as it is designed to represent an opulent yacht, complete with blond wood panelling and vintage Italian scenic prints. Choose from an extensive pasta, risotto, pizza and antipasti menu with dishes like Melanzane alla parmigiana or Chocolate Mille-feuille. There is also a breakfast menu.

Prebooking essential.

Opening hours
Monday to Friday 8am – 10.30pm
Saturday 9am – 10.30pm
Sunday 11am – 10.30pm

Nearest Underground
Notting Hill Gate 10 minutes
Bayswater 16 minutes

www.chucsrestaurants.com

Diana, Princess Of Wales Memorial Walk

Follow the heraldic rose plaques to discover places linked to Diana, Princess of Wales, during her lifetime. The seven mile route takes you past places like Kensington Palace, Buckingham Palace, St James's Palace and Spencer House, and celebrates her affection for the open spaces around her Kensington Palace home. A route map can be downloaded from the Royal Parks website, and all the plaques are easy to find.

www.royalparks.org.uk/parks/hyde-park/things-to-see-and-do/sports-and-leisure/the-diana-princess-of-wales-memorial-walk

Diana, Princess Of Wales Memorial Fountain

Hyde Park, W2 2JH

Only a few minutes walk from Kensington Palace Gardens is the Diana, Princess of Wales Memorial Fountain

on the edge of Hyde Park. Opened by Queen Elizabeth in 2004, the winding paths incorporate three bridges enabling visitors to walk to the heart of the fountain. You can sit on the edge of the fountain and dabble your feet or hands in the water, making it a lovely relaxing spot, especially on a hot day.

Opening hours are separate from rest of park
April – August: 10am – 8pm
September: 10am – 7pm
March and October: 10am – 6pm
November – February: 10am – 4pm

Nearest Underground
Knightsbridge 9 minutes

www.royalparks.org.uk/parks/hyde-park/things-to-see-and-do/memorials,-fountains-and-statues/diana

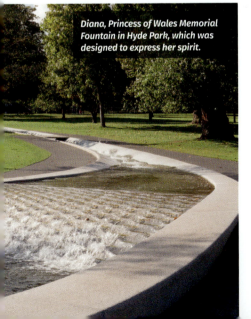

Diana, Princess of Wales Memorial Fountain in Hyde Park, which was designed to express her spirit.

Hollywood Arms
43 Hollywood Road, Kensington, SW10 9HX

Elegantly decorated in shades of blue with lots of soft furnishings, the Hollywood Arms shot to fame when the Princess of Wales was spotted joining fellow school mums for a meet and greet event, shortly after Princess Charlotte started at Thomas's school in Battersea. She is not the only Royal to appreciate the pub. Prince Harry was a frequent visitor.

A popular venue for Sunday meals and relaxing with a drink in the evening, it has its own gin and cocktail lounge on the first floor, often described as the go-to place for Chelsea socialites. It is this bar that was believed to have been hired for the meet and greet event. Apparently there is a back entrance used by VIPs.

Opening hours
11am – 11.30pm daily

Nearest Underground
Earls Court 13 minutes
West Brompton 14 minutes

www.hollywoodarmschelsea.com

Kensington Palace
Kensington Palace Gardens, W8 4PX

A royal home, museum and stunning gardens – Kensington Palace is definitely worth visiting. The Prince & Princess of Wales and their three children are by far the most famous

Kensington Palace, London, a royal palace since the seventeenth century and London home of the Prince and Princess of Wales.

modern residents, occupying a four storey apartment on one side of the Palace. For Prince William, it is a very familiar apartment since it was his childhood home with his mother, Diana Princess of Wales. Before taking up residence in the Palace itself, the Prince & Princess lived in a smaller cottage adjacent to the main building. When they moved out of the cottage, Prince Harry moved in. The Princess of Wales was often spotted taking her young children to play in Kensington Gardens or going for a walk with them. The Prince & Princess of Wales frequently undertake official engagements at Kensington Palace. President Obama for example visited them during an official state visit, and met the young Prince George before his bedtime.

Other members of the Royal Family living at Kensington Palace include the Duke and Duchess of Kent and the Duke and Duchess of Gloucester. It was the home of Diana, Princess of Wales, the Prince of Wales, the Duke of Edinburgh, Princess Margaret and Princess Eugenie and her husband, Jack Brooksbank. Queen Victoria lived here as a child, and heard the news that she had ascended to the throne while living in Kensington Palace.

William III and his Queen Mary II transformed the original Jacobean mansion on the site into a large palace. Over the years, other monarchs continued the transformation, making it into a fashionable destination.

A range of guided tours and talks are included in the entry fee to Kensington Palace, where you can explore the King's State Apartments, including the Privy Chamber, Kings Gallery and Presence Chamber. Much more intimate in scale are the Queen's Rooms, containing a staircase, gallery, closet, drawing room, dining room and bedroom. While exploring the Palace you can meet Queen Caroline and her courtiers and discover what it was like to live in eighteenth century royal society. Special exhibitions are frequently held within Kensington Palace, focusing on the lives of its various royal inhabitants as well as displays of royal clothes such as iconic items worn by Diana, Princess of Wales.

The beautiful grounds are perfect for playing, strolling and relaxation. Diana, Princess of Wales was very fond of the Sunken Garden with its pretty ornamental pond, and this was where Prince Harry and Meghan Markle held their engagement photocall for the press in 2018. A statue of Diana, Princess of Wales stands in the Sunken Garden, commissioned by her sons Prince William and Prince Harry. Interestingly, you can arrange to get married in the Orangery, or hold your reception in the Cupola Room or on the Orangery Lawn! Another popular area is the Cradle Walk with its stunning living arches made from red twigged lime.

Opening hours
10am – 6pm daily
Free access to Kensington Palace Gardens

Nearest Underground
High Street Kensington 10 minutes
Queensway 10 minutes

www.hrp.org.uk/kensington-palace

Kensington Gardens
W2 4RU

Just across the road from Kensington Palace are the Kensington Gardens. This is a royal park, created originally by Queen Caroline in 1728. Now it is a beautiful area perfect for relaxation. There are lots of flowerbeds, lawns, the Long Water, Round Pond and Broad Walk. The Serpentine boating lake forms a link with the adjacent Hyde Park. Don't miss the enchanting Elfin Oak carved with figures of fairies, elves and animals. Hunt through the gardens to find a very special statue – Peter Pan, the little boy who never grew up.

The Italian Garden is an ornamental water garden believed to have been a gift from Prince Albert to Queen Victoria, as it occupies a very similar layout to the water gardens he created at Osborne House on the Isle of Wight. The area was restored in 2011 to recreate its Victorian splendour.

For children, the most popular area in the Garden is the Diana Playground. Built as a memorial to Diana, Princess of Wales, it attracts over 1,000,000 visitors annually. It is so popular that people queue to enter on busy days in high summer. It is easy to see why it is so irresistible – children love playing in the wooden pirate ship, using the play sculptures and tepees, following the sensory trail and playing on the sand.

There are several cafés located within Kensington Gardens, and two art galleries focusing on contemporary art. Princess Eugenie was spotted attending the Serpentine Gallery's summer party with Jack Brooksbank before her marriage.

Entry is free.

Open daily dawn to dusk.

Nearest Underground
High Street Kensington 10 minutes
Queensway 10 minutes

www.royalparks.org.uk

Harrods

Brompton Road, Knightsbridge, SW1X 7XL

One of the most iconic department stores in the world, Harrods is pure luxury. Built at the turn of the twentieth century, it is a massive store covering five acres with seven floors of irresistible products, including food, cosmetics, crockery and porcelain, jewellery and designer clothes. Its toy department was the focus of Prince William's attention

The green and gold splendour of one the most iconic department stores in the world.

just before the birth of Prince George when he purchased a special Harrods bear. At one point Harrods was owned by Mohammed Al Fayed, whose son Dodi died in the Paris car crash alongside Diana, Princess of Wales. Following their deaths he installed a giant statue of the duo in the store, which stayed there for several years until Harrods was sold. At night the store is a blaze of light, with over 12,000 bulbs lighting up the exterior.

Opening hours
Monday to Saturday 10am – 9pm
Sunday 12 noon to 6pm

Nearest Underground
Knightsbridge 3 minutes

www.harrods.com

Harvey Nichols
109 – 125 Knightsbridge, SW1X 7RJ

This is another of the Princess of Wales favourite stores, as she has been photographed leaving the store on several occasions. There were reports that Diana, Princess of Wales also frequented the store. It is often referred to as 'Harvey Nicks'. Founded in 1832, it is a glamorous, luxury department store selling a wide range of international brands, designer clothing, accessories and beauty products on eight floors. The top floor of Harvey Nichols is where you can find premium food on sale, as well as some extremely upmarket restaurants. The Knightsbridge shop

Harvey Nichols is a favourite shopping venue of the Princess of Wales.

is their flagship store, focusing on desirable, cutting edge brands aiming to provide 'the ultimate fashion experience, the place to be'.

Opening hours
Monday to Saturday 10am – 8pm
Sunday 12 noon – 6pm

Nearest Underground
Knightsbridge 1 minutes
Hyde Park Corner 6 minutes

www.harveynichols.com/store/knightsbridge

High Street Kensington

W8 5ED

A popular shopping area containing many of the Princess of Wales favourite boutiques and high street stores such as Reiss, Russell and Bromley and Zara. While on tour in India, she wore a pair of Accessorise jewellery filigree earrings. In March 2020, she was seen in Waterstones buying a large bag of history and military themed books for her children. Prince Harry dropped into Nando's on the high street, and was seen in TK Maxx while Meghan Markle was seen shopping at WholeFoods and Ilapothecary. She was photographed leaving the Heidi Klein store just before her engagement to Prince Harry was announced. According to her lifestyle blog, The Tig, Kensington Flower Corner (just round the corner from the Palace) was her favourite place to buy flowers when in London. The Prince & Princess of Wales even made an unexpected Poppy Appeal appearance at High Street Kensington tube station.

Check out the adjacent Kensington Church Street for some other interesting shops such as Kensington Lighting trading as Ann's Lighting, who were lampshade makers and lighting suppliers to HM Queen Elizabeth. Gentleman's outfitters Hornets are rumoured to be the place where Kensington Palace makes deliveries from time to time. Hornets claims to be the 'oldest gentleman's vintage clothier in England.'

High Street Kensington forms part of the legendary King's Road stretching for over two miles between Sloane Square and Fulham. Named after Charles II, it was his private road when travelling to Kew in the seventeenth century. With over 300 stores, restaurants, cafés and galleries along the King's Road, it is one of London's most famous shopping streets. This is where Mary Quant and Vivienne Westwood launched 1960s Brit pop style, and the fashion element remains extremely strong.

Nearest Underground
High Street Kensington 1 minute

Launceston Place Restaurant

1A Launceston Place, W8 5RL

A discreet restaurant created from a series of small rooms, decorated with bespoke artwork by contemporary artists. This Michelin-starred restaurant was popular with Diana, Princess of Wales during the 1990s and a signature cheese soufflé was named in her honour.

Nearest Underground
High Street Kensington 7 minutes

www.launestonplace-restaurant.co.uk

National Army Museum

Royal Hospital Road, Chelsea, SW3 4HT

Many members of the Royal Family have served in the army over the years. Queen Elizabeth II was a member of the ATS at the end of the Second World War, while Prince Philip served in the Royal Navy. The Prince of Wales and Prince Harry served in the Blues and Royals, with Prince Harry serving overseas in Afghanistan. In 2017, Queen Elizabeth, accompanied by the Duke of Edinburgh and the Duke of Kent (patron of the Museum), reopened the Museum's refurbished displays. One of the items on display caught Her Majesty's attention – her own uniform from when she was honorary Brigadier of the Women's Royal Army Corps between 1949–1953. Other exhibits focus on the way the army has influenced society from fashion to films, flood defences to a Sikh warrior turban, a Boer War artillery gun, stories of the liberation of Belsen and the mystery behind a Victoria Cross found on the shores of the River Thames. Special events are held here including Victory Dances and wartime weekends plus talks on a variety of subjects like tailoring the army and British army music. Guided tours of the galleries are available.

Opening hours
10am – 5.30pm daily
Closed 25, 26 December, 1 January

Nearest Underground
Sloane Square 10 minutes

www.nam.ac.uk

Natural History Museum

South Kensington, SW7 5HD

A perennial favourite with children and adults alike! Early in 2020, the young Prince Louis was spotted admiring the dinosaurs at the Museum, accompanied by his nanny, while in 2014 Kate and William took Prince George's birthday photographs within the Butterfly House. The Princess of Wales has been patron of the Natural History Museum since April 2013 and has visited it frequently.

Opened in April 1881, it contains over eighty million specimens covering every aspect of natural history, including botany, minerology, entomology and zoology. Amazing items on display include: a cup made from a human skull found in Gough's Cave, Somerset; a chunk of gold from Australia; numerous dinosaurs; a life-size cast of a blue whale; moon rocks; and casts

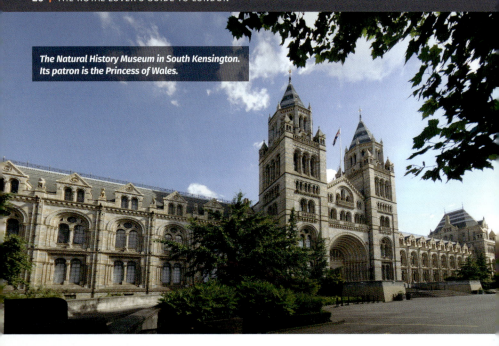

The Natural History Museum in South Kensington. Its patron is the Princess of Wales.

A life-size cast of a Blue Whale greets visitors to the Natural History Museum.

from victims of the Pompeii volcanic eruption. All the galleries are free to enter, but tickets have to be purchased for special exhibitions.

This museum forms part of a major project set up by Queen Victoria's consort, Prince Albert, in the mid-nineteenth century, to create museums offering everyone free access to history, culture, art, science and natural history.

Opening hours
10am – 5.30pm daily

Nearest Underground
South Kensington 1 minute

www.nhm.ac.uk

Partridges

2 – 5 Duke of York Square, Kings Road, Sloane Square, SW3 4LY

Holders of a Royal Warrant as Queen Elizabeth II's Grocers, Partridges is a family business selling quality food, wines and spirits from Britain and around the world. Partridges' slogan is simple: 'good things for the larder.' The store includes an outside café and a popular Saturday Fine Food market designed to support local businesses and artisans. The company has its own Partridges brand products including teas, biscuits, preserves, bags and gift items all of which display the royal warrant, and are exported worldwide.

Opening hours
8am – 10pm daily

Royal Warrant holders Partridges were suppliers to Queen Elizabeth II.

Nearest Underground
Sloane Square 3 minutes

www.partridges.co.uk

Peter Jones

Sloane Square, SW1 8EL

Set up in 1890 by a local trader called Peter Jones, the store became very successful. The *Illustrated London Magazine* described it as 'a monument to that gentleman's untiring industry and pushy enterprise'. His family were less keen, and after his death sold it to the John Lewis Group. It now holds a royal warrant as drapers and furnishers to the Prince of Wales, and did so for the Duke of Edinburgh.

The Princess of Wales has often been seen shopping for clothes as well as Christmas gifts. She was spotted browsing through racks of maternity dresses by Séraphine in 2013, and has been known to purchase the children's school shoes instore. In 2019, customers unexpectedly realised that the dark haired woman buying girls' tights was the Princess of Wales. Her mother, Carole Middleton, is said to be a Peter Jones fan. More unusually, one of Queen Elizabeth's favourite couturiers, Stewart Parvin, purchased circular lead curtain weights from Peter Jones to go inside the hems of the Queen's handmade outfits to ensure dresses did not fly up in the wind! Apart from clothes and childrenswear, Peter Jones sells beauty products, homewares, technology, sports, leisure and gifts of all kinds.

Opening hours
Monday, Tuesday, Thursday, Saturday
   9.30 – 7pm
Wednesday closes 8pm
Sunday 12 noon – 6pm

Nearest Underground
Sloane Square 2 minutes

www.johnlewis.com?our-shops/peter-jones

Portobello Road Market
Notting Hill, W11 3DB

A short walk from Kensington Gardens, this is the world's largest antique market, containing over 1,000 dealers selling every possible type of antique plus vintage clothing. Visitors come from far and wide – including Meghan Markle according to The Tig, her now defunct blog, which included many photographs she took while shopping

here. When attending her friend Misha Nonoo's wedding in 2019, Meghan was spotted wearing £5 earrings that she had borrowed from a friend who had brought them from a vintage stall on Portobello Market. Princess Beatrice is another royal who has been spotted checking out the wares of this iconic market.

The sheer size of the market means that you need to choose carefully where you head to do some shopping. Although antiques can be purchased every day, Saturday is by far the busiest and gets very crowded after 11.30am. Antiques can be found around Portobello Road and Notting Hill. Food stalls congregate around Elgin Crescent/Talbot road while vintage fashion and accessories are most evident in the Westway and Golbourne Road area. A great place to browse and find items that are unusual, chic and vintage.

On Sundays, most stalls are closed, but you can find some fashion available around Portobello Green.

Nearest Underground
Portobello Road 7 minutes

www.portobelloroad.co.uk

Royal Garden Hotel
2 – 24 Kensington High Street, W8 4PT

A luxurious hotel in the centre of Kensington High Street where the Prince and Princess of Wales welcomed the President of Singapore and his wife on an official visit. This five-star hotel contains nearly 400 bedrooms over ten floors, providing stunning views across Kensington. There are two restaurants: Park Terrace on the ground floor, and the Min Jiang restaurant on the tenth floor. Bar facilities and casual dining are available in Berties Bar and Piano Kensington.

Nearest Underground
High Street Kensington 5 minutes

www.royalgardenhotel.co.uk

Royal Hospital and RHS Chelsea Flower Show

Royal Hospital Road, SW3 4SR

This is the venue for the oldest flower show in the world – the Chelsea Flower Show. Organised by the Royal Horticultural Society, it is definitely the premier horticultural event and is guaranteed a royal presence. Queen Elizabeth was patron of the Royal Horticultural Society and rarely missed the Chelsea Flower Show. One of the very few occasions that she missed Chelsea was 1953 – when the Show took the Coronation as its theme.

Members of the Royal Family attend on a preview day. In 2019, the Princess of Wales was invited by the RHS to work with landscape designers Davies White to create the RHS show garden. The resultant entry was entitled Back to Nature, and aimed at encouraging young people and children to rediscover the natural world. Her

children joined in the preparations, helping to plant forget-me-nots. Prince Harry's Sentebale charity was involved in the creation of show gardens in 2013 and 2015.

The Chelsea Flower Show includes many *avant-garde* show gardens, artisan and urban gardens as well as being a place to buy and see new plants and garden-related products. There are usually some unusual eye catching designs: for example in 2014 life-size topiary elephants were on display. It is a popular event, attended by 157,000 people annually. Visitor numbers are strictly limited due to the size of the site and tickets have to be purchased in advance.

At other times of the year, visitors can book guided tours of the Royal Hospital and its museum. These tours are led by Chelsea Pensioners who live in the Royal Hospital. Founded by Charles II, the Royal Hospital acts as a retirement home and nursing home for over 300 British army veterans, who are instantly recognisable by their iconic red uniforms.

On Founders Day, 29 May, a member of the Royal Family visits the Hospital to review the Pensioners. Queen Consort Camilla undertook the review in 2013, the Earl of Wessex in 2017, Prince Michael of Kent in 2018 and the Duke of Sussex in 2019.

Nearest Underground
Sloane Square 8 minutes

www.chelsea-pensioners.co.uk

Royal Albert Hall

Kensington Gore, SW7 2BX

A premier music and entertainment venue in London, it has been attracting visitors since Victorian times. Numerous royal events have been held here, including Queen Elizabeth II ninety-second birthday party involving music and song from across the Commonwealth. In March 2020, the Duke and Duchess of Sussex attended one of their final official engagements when they attended the Mountbatten Festival of Music, with Harry acting for the last time as Captain General of the Royal Marines. By far the most well known royal event held at the Royal Albert Hall is the annual Royal British Legion Festival of Remembrance. Attended by members of the Royal Family including King Charles, Queen Consort Camilla, the Prince and Princess of Wales, the Earl and Countess of Wessex and the Princess Royal, the festival commemorates all those who have lost their lives in battle. It culminates in a dramatic fall of poppies from the great dome high overhead.

The Royal Albert Hall is named in honour of Prince Albert, consort to Queen Victoria. The Prince had been instrumental in creating a massive cultural area within Kensington involving museums as well as the

The Royal Albert Hall is the venue for concerts and events such as the Royal British Legion Festival of Remembrance attended by the Royal Family.

music and arts venue. A statue of Prince Albert can be seen in the Albert Memorial outside. Numerous events are held at the Royal Albert Hall throughout the year, including the annual BBC Proms concerts. The Prince and Princess of Wales made a private visit to watch a performance of Cirque du Soleil in 2020.

You can book guided tours of the building most days of the week. Booking in advance is essential. The tours take you behind the scenes providing an opportunity to see parts of the Hall not normally open to the public, and to follow a special interest such as architecture, film and TV, or to enable visitors to learn about its history and see the royal box.

Nearest Underground
South Kensington 15 minutes
High Street Kensington 15 minutes

www.royalalberthall.com

San Lorenzo

22 Beauchamp Place, Knightsbridge, SW3 1NH

Princess Diana was fond of dining out, and San Lorenzo was a favourite lunch spot. She would take William and Harry to lunch at the restaurant. San Lorenzo has always been known as a popular celebrity venue attracting people like Joan Collins and Jack Nicholson. San Lorenzo is a large restaurant with six private dining rooms, specialising in traditional Italian cuisine combining Tuscan, Piedmontese and Roman influences. Ingredients are locally sourced. Typical dishes include Pecorino Salad and Spaghetti all'Aragosta, and Affrogato al caffe.

Opening hours
Monday to Saturday 12.30 – 3pm then 6.30 – 10pm

Nearest Underground
Knightsbridge 9 minutes
South Kensington 12 minutes

www.sanlorenzolondon.co.uk

Science Museum

Exhibition Road, South Kensington, SW7 2DD

Founded in 1857 by Prince Albert and Queen Victoria, the royal links have been continuously maintained. Queen Elizabeth made her first visit to the museum in 1939, when she and her sister Princess Margaret accompanied their grandmother Queen Mary on a visit exploring the museum. In 2014, Queen Elizabeth II opened the Information Age gallery by sending a royal Tweet. Five years later in 2019, Queen Elizabeth came to open the Supporters' Centre and sent an Instagram post, having been shown letters on display between Charles Babbage and her great, great grandfather Prince Albert concerning the Difference Engine now on display in the Making of the Modern World gallery.

Explore the making of the modern world and how life has changed.

Apollo 10 capsule on display in the Science Museum Kensington.

This is a museum containing some amazing items, including Stephenson's Rocket, the Apollo 10 rocket capsule, the Newcomen Steam Engine and Puffing Billy – the oldest surviving steam engine in the world. Over 15,000 items are on display in the museum – a fraction of its total holding of over 300,000 items.

Many of the galleries are interactive, allowing visitors to get hands-on with science discoveries, take part in science debates, blast into space and discover what it is like to fly with the legendary Red Arrows RAF aerobatic team.

Discover the science of driverless cars at the Science Museum.

There is no charge to visit the various galleries, but tickets must be purchased for special exhibitions.

Opening hours
10am – 6pm daily

Nearest Underground
South Kensington 1 minute

www.sciencemuseum.org.uk

Stewart Parvin

9 Motcomb Street, SW1X 8LB

Stewart Parvin was couturier to Queen Elizabeth between 2007 -2022, creating many of her outfits. She wore a Stewart Parvin A-line Airforce blue coat and matching hat with orange feathers to the Commonwealth service 2020 at Westminster Abbey, which marked the final official event attended by the Duke and Duchess of Sussex.

Parvin was the bookmakers' favourite to design Meghan Markle's dress in 2018, and designed the ivory silk bridal dress worn by Zara Tindell (daughter of the Princess Royal) at her wedding in 2011.

The Stewart Parvin boutique containing a range of day and evening wear is open by appointment only to view the collections.

Nearest Underground
Knightsbridge 7 minutes

www.stewartparvin.com

Tate Britain

Millbank, SW1P 4RG

Opened in 1897, The Tate is a national gallery of primarily British art, holding historical and contemporary works by artists like Hogarth, Constable, Blake, Millais, Rex Whistler, Reynolds, Stubbs, Hockney and many others from 1500 to the present day. There is a changing programme of events and exhibitions alongside the permanent collections. It was used for the 150th anniversary of the Press Association in 2018, which was attended by Prince Charles, Prince of Wales and the Duchess of Cornwall. Princess Eugenie created an Instagram post about the Hockney exhibition which was held here.

At the end of the twentieth century, the collection was divided between the original site at Millbank and the transformed iconic former power station located at Bankside, in south London. Queen Elizabeth formally opened the new extension at Bankside in 2000.

Entrance free, but special exhibitions and events may incur a charge

Opening hours
10am – 6pm daily

Nearest Underground
Pimlico 7 minutes

www.tate.org.uk

Victoria and Albert Museum

Cromwell Road, SW7 2RL

The Princess of Wales has been patron of the V&A, and its Museum of Childhood offshoot, since 2018. She is its first royal patron, reflecting her

Tate Britain is the national gallery of British Art, located in Millbank.

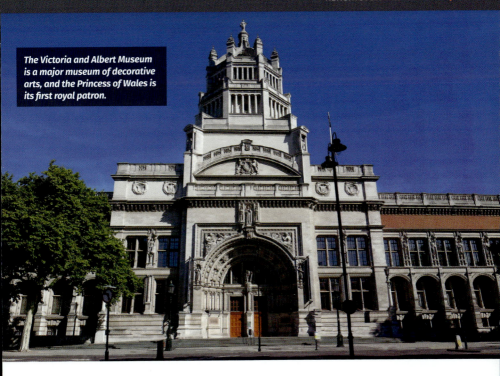

The Victoria and Albert Museum is a major museum of decorative arts, and the Princess of Wales is its first royal patron.

interest in the visual arts, photography, design and childhood.

In 2017, she unveiled the new Exhibition Road Quarter, and opened the Photography Gallery. During her tour, she visited the jewellery gallery to see the unique Victoria coronet, and tried out the stereoscopic viewer to see photographs taken by women in the 1850s.

Princesses Beatrice and Eugenie are frequent visitors at the museum, especially for the opening of new exhibitions. According to Princess Eugenie's Instagram site, the Raphael Cartoon Room at the V&A is 'unmissable'.

Founded by Queen Victoria and Prince Albert, The V&A contains over 2.27m items and is the world's largest museum of applied and decorative arts. On display are over 5,000 years of artworks, including costumes, textiles, silver, ironwork, jewellery, furniture, sculpture, prints and photographs. There is a large East and South Asian collection, as well as an Islamic collection.

Entry to the galleries is free, but payment is required to enter the exhibitions.

Opening hours
10am – 5.30pm daily

Nearest Underground
South Kensington 1 minute

www.vam.ac.uk

WESTMINSTER

Banqueting House

Whitehall, SW1A 2ER

Historically, the Banqueting House is best known for being where Charles I was beheaded in 1649 on a specially built scaffold erected just outside the building. A special service is held on the spot every year.

This is the only building that remains of the original Palace of Whitehall, used by the monarchy for centuries. A rambling, massive palace, it was destroyed by fire at the end of the seventeenth century. Built on the orders of Charles I, the Banqueting House was used primarily as a venue for royal entertainment. Its most spectacular feature is the ceiling, which includes paintings by Rubens. Nowadays, it is used mainly as a venue for charities and organisations holding large events, often attended by members of the Royal Family, for example the Prince & Princess of Wales were guests of honour at the Tusk Conservation Awards.

Open to the public via guided tours

Nearest Underground
Charing Cross 6 minutes
Embankment 10 minutes

Nearest Train
Charing Cross 6 minutes

www.hrp.org.uk

Buckingham Palace

The Mall, SW1A 1AA

This is definitely one of the most famous, and most photographed buildings in the world, and is instantly recognisable. Buckingham Palace is the official residence of King Charles III – and you can tell immediately whether he is in London by checking the flag flying over the Palace.

If the Royal Standard is flying high, then he is in London. If the Union Flag is flying, then he is at one of his other homes elsewhere in the country.

Buckingham Palace is massive. There are 775 rooms, 19 state rooms, 52 royal and guest bedrooms, 188 staff bedrooms, 92 offices and 78 bathrooms! Over 50,000 people visit the Palace every year to take part in official events hosted by the King or other members of the Royal Family, including banquets, lunches, dinners, receptions and garden parties. The King holds a weekly audience with the Prime Minister at Buckingham Palace, and

Buckingham Palace is the official London residence of King Charles III.

meets foreign ambassadors and leaders of countries taking part in state visits. Some members of the Royal Family also have apartments in the Palace, such as the Princess Royal. Although filmed at Windsor, Queen Elizabeth II's Platinum Jubilee film with Paddington Bear and marmalade sandwiches was set at Buckingham Palace. Typical events that have taken place here include a reception marking the UK Africa Summit in March 2020 hosted by the Duke and Duchess of Cambridge (now Prince and Princess of Wales), the Princess Royal and the Countess of Wessex. The same month saw the Duchess of Cambridge hosting a gala dinner party for the twenty-fifth anniversary of the charity Place2Be. President Trump attended a state dinner at the Palace during his official visit in 2019. It was here that King Charles, the Queen Consort Camilla, the Prince & Princess of Wales held a reception for world leaders attending

The royal standard of King Charles III flies above Buckingham Palace when he is in London.

the funeral of Queen Elizabeth II in September 2022.

Following her death at Balmoral, Scotland, Queen Elizabeth's coffin was brought to Buckingham Palace where it stayed overnight in the historic Bow Room before the formal lying in state at Westminster Hall. After the funeral, a gun carriage bearing the coffin was pulled by Royal Navy sailors past Buckingham Palace, with staff coming out to pay their regards.

Buckingham Palace has been the official home of UK monarchs since 1837, when Queen Victoria moved in. George II had originally purchased the building in 1761 for his wife, Queen Charlotte, to use as a family home. Queen Victoria extended the building to add a fourth wing, and the façade was later redone in 1913 using Portland stone. Queen Victoria lived in Buckingham Palace with her beloved husband, Prince Albert of Saxe-Coburg Gotha until he died of typhoid in December 1861. Queen Victoria fled from London, seeking seclusion at Windsor Castle, blaming the bad drainage of London for her husband's death. For the next ten years, she spent very little time at Buckingham Palace.

The great balcony at the front is where the King and working members of the Royal Family appear on special occasions such as the Trooping the Colour, the seventy-fifth anniversary of the Battle of Britain and royal weddings such as that of the Prince William and Kate Middleton. The central gate is only used for state occasions, while the north centre gate has become the everyday entrance used by all visitors to the palace, including royalty.

The front courtyard is the venue for the regular Changing of the Guard ceremony during which the King's Guard hands over responsibility for

The ceremony of Changing of the Guard outside Buckingham Palace.

protecting the Palace to a New Guard. The ceremony takes place daily during June and July, while between August and May it takes place on Mondays, Wednesdays, Fridays and Sundays. It lasts about 45 minutes, but if you want a good view it is best to arrive early, as it is very popular.

The New Guard march from Wellington Barracks in Birdcage Walk, arriving at Buckingham Palace at 11am, where the Old Guard have formed up in the courtyard, having been joined by a detachment from St James's Palace. The military band plays the regimental slow march as the New Guard arrive and take their places, facing the Old Guard. The officer in charge of the Old Guard symbolically hands over the keys to the palace to represent the transfer of responsibility, salutes and the New Guard begins to post new sentries. When the handover is complete, the Old Guard marches out back to Wellington Barracks. The New Guard divides, with half of the soldiers marching down the Mall to take position at St James's Palace. During the ceremony, the bands play a variety of military and non-military music – and have been known to play *Happy Birthday* on the King's birthday.

Buckingham Palace is open to the public for pre-booked guided tours during the summer, plus limited entry in December and at Easter. There is a timed entrance system which is strictly maintained. During the tour, you can visit nineteen State rooms, including the White Drawing Room, Throne Room, Picture Gallery, Ballroom, Grand Staircase. All the rooms are laid out ready for a State Visit and there are many items from the Royal Collection on display, including antique furniture, ceramics and paintings by Rembrandt, Rubens and Poussin. The tour ends in the beautiful gardens of the Palace, which have been described as a 'walled oasis in the middle of London' as they include flowerbeds, lawns, lake plus extensive woodland and wild flower areas.

Nearest Underground
Victoria 10 minutes
Westminster 10 – 15 minutes via
    St James's Park
Green Park 10 minutes

Mainline Train
Victoria 10 minutes

www.rct.uk/visit/the-state-rooms-buckingham-palace

Cenotaph
Whitehall, SW1A 2ET

Designed by Edwin Lutyens, the Cenotaph was unveiled on 11 November 1920 as a symbol of remembrance for all those who had died during the First World War. It is now the official memorial for all those who died in both World Wars, as well as members of the British military forces who have been killed in subsequent wars such as Korea and Iraq. Constructed from white

The Cenotaph following the Remembrance Day wreath-laying ceremony attended by King Charles III and senior members of the Royal Family.

Portland stone, it forms a tall pylon made from gradually diminishing tiers on top of an empty tomb, surmounted by a laurel wreath. On the side are written the words The Glorious Dead, flanked by flags.

The Cenotaph is the location of the National Service of Remembrance held at 11am on Remembrance Sunday (the Sunday closest to the 11 November Armistice Day when fighting in the First World War came to an end). A very sombre event, it involves members of the Royal Family and Government laying wreaths at the Cenotaph. The King, the Prince of Wales, the Princess Royal and the Earl of Wessex lay wreaths during the ceremony. The Queen Consort, Princess of Wales and the Countess of Wessex watch the ceremony from the balcony of the Foreign and Commonwealth Office, sited directly opposite the Cenotaph. The Duchess of Sussex joined them in 2019. After all the wreaths have been laid, there is a two minute silence before a trumpeter sounds the evocative Last Post and then over 10,000 veterans march past the Cenotaph.

Nearest Underground
Charing Cross 6 minutes
Embankment 10 minutes

Nearest Train
Charing Cross 6 minutes

www.english-heritage.org.uk/visit/places/the-cenotaph

Clarence House

8 Cleveland Row, St James's, SW1A 1BA

Clarence House is only open to visitors during August. Tickets have to be pre-booked and allow you to see the five ground floor reception rooms where official engagements are undertaken, as well as the garden and items from the Royal Collection.

This is the London home of King Charles and the Queen Consort Camilla while Buckingham Palace is undergoing major maintenance works. As a result the Royal Standard also flies over Clarence House. A splendid white stone Georgian building, it stands beside St James's Palace facing onto the Mall. It has been a royal home for many years, having been the first home of Queen Elizabeth II (then Princess Elizabeth) and the Duke of Edinburgh following their marriage in 1947. When Princess Elizabeth became Queen, she moved to Buckingham Palace and Queen Elizabeth, the Queen Mother moved to Clarence House living here until her death in 2002. While Prince of Wales, King Charles held numerous events and receptions, and entertained official visitors to the UK such as the Dalai Lama in 2012. There are large gardens at the back of the Clarence House, which are shared with St James's Palace. Prince William stayed here the night before his wedding, along with Prince Harry. Speaking on the documentary *'Elizabeth: Queen, Wife, Mother'* he later recalled that the crowds on the Mall 'were singing and cheering all night long, so the excitement of that, the nervousness of me and everyone singing – I slept for about half an hour.'

Nearest Underground
St James's Park 5 minutes
Piccadilly Circus 8 minutes

Mainline Train
Charing Cross 10 minutes

www.royal.uk/royal-residences-clarence-house

Goring Hotel

15 Beeston Place, London, SW1W 0JW

Forbes Travel Guide describes The Goring Hotel as being 'the most glamorous accommodation option in England.' It is a family run hotel, and is the closest hotel to Buckingham Palace. This is where Kate Middleton spent the final night before her wedding to Prince William in 2011. The Middleton family booked all seventy-one rooms at the hotel to accommodate their friends and family. Kate and her immediate family stayed on the fifth floor of the luxury hotel. Kate herself occupied the Royal Suite comprising a bedroom, sitting room, dining room, bathroom and guest cloakroom. The suite is furnished with antique furniture, and contains many unique royal items including hand written letters and military regalia. Protected by aircraft safety glass, a life size portrait of Queen Victoria adorns the shower of the bathroom, while the walls are lined with silk matching the throne room in Buckingham Palace. The Royal Suite's balcony runs along the entire length of the top floor, and overlooks the Goring gardens. A Goring footman is on call 24/7 whenever the suite is occupied.

It is said that eight hours before the wedding, Prince Harry (the best man) partied at the hotel, finally leaving it by jumping off a balcony – which resulted in him landing badly on his ankle.

The Goring Hotel is a firm favourite of the Royal Family. In 2013, it received a royal warrant – the only hotel to possess such a warrant for the provision of hospitality services. The Princess of Wales has been known to visit the hotel for afternoon tea, while Queen Elizabeth II used to host Christmas lunch here for senior members of her staff. The Queen Mother was a frequent visitor, dining on Eggs Drumkilbo (a lobster and egg based dish). At the end of the Second World War, the King, Queen and Princesses Elizabeth and Margaret came over to the Goring Hotel to celebrate.

Nearest Underground
Victoria 3 minutes

Nearest Train
Victoria 3 minutes

www.thegoring.com

Green Park and Hyde Park

Two Royal Parks adjacent to Buckingham Palace, these are the traditional venues for various royal gun salutes fired by the Royal Horse Artillery. It is a spectacular sight with teams of horses pulling guns galloping across the park, setting up and firing within minutes. The guns are always fired at midday and take place on state visits, the state opening of Parliament, the birthdays of the King and the Prince of Wales as well as Remembrance Sunday. Similar gun salutes are used to celebrate special events such as royal Jubilees or the birth of the Prince of Wales children: George, Charlotte and Louis.

The Household Cavalry ride through the park regularly on their way to the Changing of the Guard ceremony at Horse Guards Parade.

Prior to the funeral of Queen Elizabeth II, Green Park was the site of a temporary memorial garden hosting thousands of floral tributes, with a secondary site being eventually added in Hyde Park.

Following the funeral service at Westminster Abbey, the Queen's coffin was placed on a gun carriage pulled by a large team of Royal Navy sailors from the Abbey to Wellington Arch at Hyde Park Corner. The route passed Buckingham Palace and then followed the road between the Palace Gardens and Green Park. The coffin was then transferred to the State Hearse to travel to Windsor. A Royal Gun Salute was given by the Kings Troup, Royal Horse Artillery in Hyde

Park, as the State Hearse departed from Wellington Arch along the South Carriage Ride to the Albert Memorial.

Take a look at the massive Queen Elizabeth Gate, which was installed to commemorate the ninetieth birthday of Queen Elizabeth the Queen Mother. The central screen unites two national symbols: the lion of England with the unicorn of Scotland reflecting her role in England, and her Scottish birthplace.

Both parks provide a great place to relax and stroll, especially in the summertime. The Serpentine Lake is a popular venue with swimmers, as well as offering the opportunity to take a boat out. At Christmas, Hyde Park hosts one of the largest Christmas markets in the UK together with an ice rink and funfair.

Nearest Underground
Hyde Park Corner 1 minute
Green Park 1 minute

www.royalparks.org.uk/parks/green-park/things-to-see-and-do/events-in-green-park/royal-gun-salutes

Guards Museum

Wellington Barracks, Birdcage Walk, SW1E 6HQ

This is the regimental museum of the five regiments of Footguards responsible for guarding the King. These are the Grenadier Guards, Coldstream Guards, Scots Guards, Irish Guards and Welsh Guards. It acts as a living museum to the thousands of guardsmen who have served in these regiments since the formation of the Coldstream Guards in 1660. Apart from their role protecting the sovereign and the royal palaces, which includes taking part in ceremonies such as the Changing of the Guard and Trooping the Colour, the Guards are active soldiers serving in all major campaigns and wars across the centuries. Memorabilia relating to those campaigns and the activities of the various Guards regiments can be seen in the museum. The King is Colonel-in-chief of the Guards regiments, The Prince of Wales is Colonel of the Welsh Guards, the Princess of Wales Colonel of the Irish Guards, and Prince Edward, Duke of Kent, is Colonel of the Scots Guards.

VIP tours can be arranged at an extra cost, providing a personal and immersive experience, meeting soldiers of the guard, with a guided tour and special photo opportunities.

Entry charge

Opening hours
10am – 4pm daily

Nearest Underground
St James's Park 8 minutes
Westminster 9 minutes

www.theguardsmuseum.com

Horse Guards Parade

Horse Guards, SW1A 2HQ

Horse Guards Parade is a large parade ground located between Whitehall

Horse Guards Parade is where the Trooping of the Colour ceremony, attended by King Charles III and senior members of the Royal Family, is held each year.

and St James's Park. It is the venue for the annual Trooping of the Colour celebrating the monarch's birthday. Dating back to the seventeenth century, this is an event involving a lot of pageantry, colour and precision marching by the participating soldiers. Over 1,000 soldiers parade before their sovereign, together with 200 mounted cavalry, plus 200 musicians from six military bands and the corps of drums. In total there are 113 words of command given by the officer in charge of the parade. Five regiments of foot guards are involved in the event – the Grenadier Guards, Coldstream Guards, Scots Guards, Irish Guards, Welsh Guards. These five regiments take it in turn to 'troop' their colour, a different regiment taking priority each year.

The King either rides a horse or uses a carriage to travel from Buckingham Palace via the Mall and Horse Guards Road to the Parade ground. Other carriages within the procession contain members of the Royal Family such as Queen Consort Camilla, the Princess of Wales and the Countess of Wessex. The Royal Colonels - the Prince of Wales (Welsh Guards), Princess Royal (Blues & Royals) Duke of Kent (Scots Guards) ride on horseback directly behind the King in the procession.

The procession arrives at exactly 11am. The King takes the salute, and the

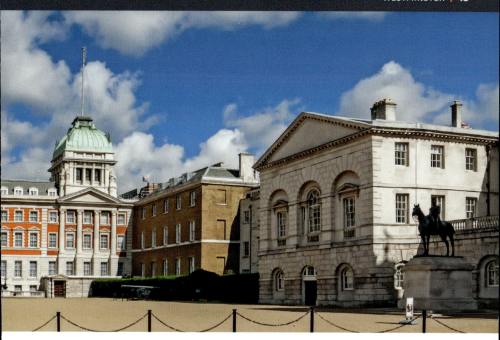

The colourful pageantry of the Trooping the Colour ceremony at Horse Guards.

parade begins with an inspection, during which the King passes down the ranks of all five regiments and the Household Cavalry. After returning to Buckingham Palace, the Royal Family stand on the balcony to watch an RAF flypast.

The Beating of the Retreat ceremony is held on the Wednesday and Thursday evening immediately prior to the Trooping of the Colour. A member of the Royal Family attends one of the evenings. Prince Harry attended in 2017, Prince William in 2018 and the Princess of Wales 2019. This evening pageant involves a programme of music and military precision, cannons and fireworks. It lasts about one hour and thirty minutes.

On a daily basis, this is the venue for the Changing of the Kings Life Guard featuring the Household Cavalry Mounted Regiment, comprising the Life Guards (red tunics with white plumed helmets), and the Blues and Royals (blue tunics and red plumed helmets). The Life Guards have maintained a guard at Horse Guards, representing the official entrance to both St James's Palace and Buckingham Palace, since 1660, when Charles II was restored to the throne.

During the Changing of the King's Life Guard ceremony, the new Guard leaves Hyde Park Barracks at 10.28am (weekdays) or 9.28am (Sundays) to ride to Whitehall via Hyde Park Corner, Constitution Hill and The Mall. The ceremony lasts approximately 30 minutes. It starts at 11am weekdays, or 10am on Sundays. The Old Guard forms up on the North Side of the Horse Guards enclosure. When the New Guard arrives, trumpeters sound the royal salute and the New Guard forms up opposite the Old Guard. The Old Guard sentries join the rest of the Old Guard, and depart. The New Guard rides through the arch, dismounts and horses are led to the stables. Mounted sentries are placed at the entrance to Horse Guards, and change every hour or half-hour in winter until 4pm when a dismounting ceremony takes place.

Interestingly, no cars or carriages can pass through Horse Guards arch unless the traveller has an official Ivory Pass. The only exemptions from the rule are members of the Royal Family. In September 2022, the Funeral Procession of Queen Elizabeth II left Westminster Abbey, travelled up Whitehall, before passing through Horse Guards Arch and across Horse Guards Parade, then along Horse Guards Road to the Mall.

Pre-booked tickets are required for the Trooping of the Colour and Beating the Retreat ceremonies.

Changing of the Guard ceremony – free of charge

Nearest Underground
Charing Cross 6 minutes
St James Park 10 minutes

Nearest Train
Charing Cross 6 minutes

Household Cavalry Museum

Horse Guards, Whitehall, SW1A 2HQ

This is a small but fun museum where you can find out about the history and work of the Household Cavalry whether on ceremonial duties or in combat. If you arrive when the museum opens you can watch the horses being prepared and the troopers mounting up, before watching the Changing of the Guard ceremony. Afterwards you can return to the museum to finish your tour, and watch the troopers tending to the horses within the working stables.

The Princess Royal is Colonel of the Blues and Royals, the second most senior regiment in the British Army. Prince William was commissioned and served in the Blues and Royals, before moving to the RAF Search and Rescue Force as a helicopter pilot. Prince Harry served in the Blues and Royals on active service as an Armoured Reconnaissance Troop Leader and wore its official dress uniform at his wedding to Meghan Markle in 2018.

Entry charge

Opening hours
April – October 10am – 6pm
November – March 10am – 5pm
Closed July 20, December 24, 25, 26

Nearest Underground
Charing Cross 6 minutes
St James's Park 10 minutes

Nearest Train
Charing Cross 6 minutes

www.householdcavalrymuseum.co.uk

Houses of Parliament

Parliament Square, SW1A 2JR

More correctly, this is the Palace of Westminster comprising the House of Commons, House of Lords, Westminster Hall and Elizabeth Tower housing the famous Big Ben clock.

Most of the buildings on the site date from the late nineteenth century.

Standing guard at Horse Guards.

Big Ben and the Palace of Westminster with the Houses of Parliament, seen from the River Thames.

In October 1834, the majority of the original medieval palace was destroyed in a great fire, due to the burning of small wooden tally sticks used by the Exchequer for hundreds of years, which ignited the panelling in the Lords Chamber! A major rebuilding programme resulted in the construction of the building we know today.

One of the few medieval buildings that survived the fire was Westminster Hall. This is in daily use by people visiting the Houses of Parliament. The Hall is also used for various ceremonial and state occasions. This is where Queen Elizabeth II's coffin lay in state prior to the funeral in Westminster Abbey. It was guarded by soldiers from the Sovereign's Bodyguard, along with Foot Guards and members of the Household Cavalry Mounted Regiment. It was here that the two Princes Vigils were held – one by the King, Princess Royal, Prince Andrew and Prince Edward; the other by the grandchildren led by the Prince of Wales. More than a quarter of a million people filed past her coffin during the four-day period.

In 2002, Queen Elizabeth The Queen Mother lay in state here for three days

before her funeral. Over 200,000 people filed past to pay their last respects. When celebrating her Diamond Jubilee in 2012, Queen Elizabeth II addressed both Houses of Parliament in Westminster Hall.

The State Opening of Parliament is a major ceremonial occasion when the monarch announces the government's plans for the coming year. It is a very colourful ceremony. Before the King arrives, the building is officially searched for gunpowder – a tradition dating back to the seventeenth century Gunpowder Plot when Guy Fawkes attempted to blow up the Palace of Westminster. On arriving at the Houses of Parliament, the King is escorted to the Robing Room where he dons his official robes and crown. He then walks to the House of Lords to ascend the throne. Members of the House of Commons are summoned to hear his speech, leaving one of their members as a 'hostage', who is released as soon as the King leaves the Houses of Parliament!

The monarch is not allowed to enter the House of Commons. This is strictly forbidden due to a long-held parliamentary convention dating back to the seventeenth century. King Charles I forced his way into the House of Commons in an attempt to arrest five Members of Parliament for treason – they had already fled. After this, it became accepted practice that the monarch could not enter the House of Commons.

Visitors to the Houses of Parliament can take part in behind the scenes guided tours which take you around the main areas, including the Lobby, Westminster Hall, House of Commons and House of Lords, where you can see the stunning golden thrones used by the King and his consort, as well as the Chairs of State used by the

The Houses of Parliament, in the Palace of Westminster, where the King attends the State Opening of Parliament.

Prince & Princess of Wales, whenever they accompany the King to the State Opening of the Houses of Parliament.

It is not possible to watch the actual State Opening of Parliament, but you can watch the royal procession to and from Buckingham Palace to the Houses of Parliament. This is a colourful and dramatic sight, as the King travels in the ornate Irish State Coach, accompanied by mounted detachments of the Household Cavalry.

Guided tours of the Houses of Parliament must be pre-booked. There is a charge. When the House is in session, members of the public can watch the debates free of charge.

Opening hours
Daily for pre-booked guided tours

Nearest Underground
Westminster 2 minutes

www.parliament.uk/visiting

The Mall
Westminster, SW1A 2WH

Stretching from Buckingham Palace to Admiralty Arch near Trafalgar Square, The Mall is the main ceremonial route for royal processions and special events such as royal weddings, funerals, jubilees and of course the coronation when the King used the Gold State coach to travel between Buckingham Palace and Westminster Abbey. It is used by soldiers taking part in the Changing of the Guard ceremonies at Buckingham Palace, St James's Palace and Horse Guards Parade. Prince William and Kate Middleton rode in carriages along the Mall after their wedding to reach Buckingham Palace, where they appeared on the famous balcony – as did the Prince of Wales and Diana, Princess of Wales many years earlier.

The Mall looking towards Buckingham Palace, ready for a State event.

In September 2022, it formed part of the funeral procession of Queen Elizabeth II following the service in Westminster Abbey. The gun carriage on which her coffin rested was pulled by Royal Navy sailors along the Mall, followed in procession by the King and other members of the Royal Family.

The wide avenue is lined with trees and buildings set well back from the street, while on the other side of the road is St James's Park.

Nearest Underground
St James's Park 5 minutes

Queen's Gallery

Buckingham Palace, SW1A 1AA

Located adjacent to Buckingham Palace, the Queen's Gallery offers a fantastic opportunity to see some of the spectacular artworks held within the Royal Collection. Queen Elizabeth II opened the Gallery during the 2002 Golden Jubilee celebrations. There is a changing programme of exhibitions; for example a Fabergé exhibition, which included a host of little animals and one of the legendary eggs. The Royal Collection includes works by all major artists including Canaletto, Rubens, Rembrandt, Constable and Leonardo Da Vinci.

Open daily. Tickets can be purchased purely for the Queen's Gallery. During the summer, combined tickets entitled A Royal Day Out are available which include access to the State Rooms at Buckingham Palace, the Queen's Gallery and the Royal Mews.

Nearest Underground
Victoria 10 minutes
Green Park 10 minutes

Mainline Train
Victoria 10 minutes

www.rct.uk

Quagliano's Restaurant

16 Bury St., St James, SW1 6AY

Follow in royal footsteps and enjoy contemporary European food and cocktails for a superb dining experience. Typical dishes on offer include confit duck leg, pomme Lyonnaise, pied du mouton mushrooms, heritage kale, salted grapes, sauce Veronique.

This was the first public restaurant ever visited by a reigning monarch when Queen Elizabeth II and Prince Philip dined here in 1956 to celebrate the British equestrian team's medal at the Stockholm Olympics. Over the next decades, both Prince Philip and Princess Margaret dined here regularly. Princess Margaret went so often that the restaurant permanently reserved a table for her exclusive use. Princess Diana was another frequent visitor, although she usually arrived by sneaking through the kitchen to avoid the paparazzi. Prior to his marriage, Prince Harry was a regular customer, accompanied by his friends and numerous pretty girls!

Nearest Underground
Green Park 5 minutes
Piccadilly 6 minutes

www.quaglinos-restaurant.co.uk

Royal Mews

Buckingham Palace, SW1W OQH

Ever wondered what those carriages are really like when you see the King and other members of the Royal Family driving in ceremonial processions? Now is your chance to find out. Just to the left of Buckingham Palace is the entry to the Royal Mews where all these amazing coaches are kept. By far the most spectacular is the Gold State Coach, which is used at every coronation. It is immensely heavy, weighing four tonnes, and needs eight horses to pull it. Apparently, it is also very uncomfortable! While being interviewed in 2018, Queen Elizabeth II commented that riding in the coach was 'a horrible experience' since 'it is only sprung on leather and can only go at a walking pace.' When she sat in the coach, she was very high up, much higher than the coachmen several feet below! The coach was used during Queen Elizabeth II Platinum Jubilee celebrations in 2022, and for the coronation of King Charles III in 2023. Other coaches on display include the Glass Coach used by Diana, Princess

of Wales on her way to her wedding in St Paul's Cathedral; the horse drawn Landau used by the Prince & Princess of Wales after their wedding ceremony, and the Ascot Landau used by Prince Harry and Meghan following their wedding in Windsor. For a more modern touch, there is a Rolls Royce bearing the Royal insignia used on numerous occasions, including taking Kate Middleton to Westminster Abbey on her wedding day. While at the Royal Mews, you can step into a replica semi-state Landau, see the horses in their stables, view an eighteenth century riding school and the elaborate harnesses worn by the horses.

Entry charge

Opening hours
10am – 5pm daily

Nearest Underground
Victoria 10 minutes
Westminster 10 – 15 minutes via
    St James's Park
Green Park 10 minutes

Mainline Train
Victoria 10 minutes

www.rct.uk/visit/the-royal-mews

St James's Park

The Mall, SW1A 2BJ

A royal park, it originally formed part of the gardens of St James's Palace. It is the oldest of all the royal parks in London. St James's Park is a very relaxing place to stroll, with pretty flowerbeds, lake and expansive lawns. St James's Park includes the Victoria Memorial and the famous brightly coloured flowerbeds in front of Buckingham Palace. Scarlet geraniums make a brilliant splash of colour each summer to match the red of the Guards' uniforms, while in the spring there are masses of scarlet tulips. On the far side of St James's Park, it backs on to the wide expanse of Horse Guards Parade where the Trooping of the Colour takes place each June.

Nearest Underground
St James's Park 5 minutes

www.royalparks.org.uk/parks/st-james-park

St James's Palace

Marlborough Road, The Mall, SW1A 1BQ

The senior royal palace within the UK, it is home to several members of the Royal Family and contains numerous Royal Household offices. Princes William and Harry had their offices here before moving to Kensington Palace. It is the London residence of the Princess Royal and Princess Alexandra, and is the location of several Royal organisations such as the Yeomen of the Guard, Queens Watermen and the Royal Collection Trust. The state apartments are frequently used for entertaining during state visits and other formal events. In February 2020, the Prince of

St James's Palace – a Tudor royal castle which remains the official home of the royal court.

Wales held a reception here marking 150 years of the Metropolitan and City Police Orphans Fund.

St James's Palace was a royal residence for over 300 years, until Queen Victoria moved to Buckingham Palace. Henry VIII ordered its construction between 1531–1536, and much of the Tudor palace remains, including the Chapel Royal. Queen Elizabeth I lived here during the threat posed by the potential invasion of the Spanish Armada in 1588, and Queen Victoria married Prince Albert in the Chapel Royal at St James's Palace in 1840. Prince George, Princess Charlotte and Prince Louis were christened in the Chapel Royal and Diana, Princess of Wales lay in state here before her funeral. The Chapel Royal is unusual in that it is a Royal Peculiar – answerable only to the King.

St James's Palace is the site of one very key ceremonial function – it is where the Accession Council meets following the death of a monarch as happened in September 2022. The Privy Council met here to declare King Charles as the new monarch with the Prince of Wales being the first to sign the proclamation. The King signed the oath of accession, witnessed by the Prince of Wales. The Garter King of Arms officially announced the accession of a new sovereign from the Proclamation Gallery, above Friary Court.

Ambassadors are still officially credited to the Court of St James, not to Buckingham Palace.

The Palace is not open to the public.

Nearest Underground
Charing Cross 6 minutes
Piccadilly Circus 8 minutes

Mainline Train
Charing Cross 6 minutes

www.royal.uk/royal-residences

Spencer House

27 St James's Place, SW1A 1NR

Built as the London home for the Earls of Althorp and the Spencer family, it is the only eighteenth century aristocratic palace to remain intact. It is still owned by the Spencer family, of whom Diana, Princess of Wales, was a member. Her brother, Charles, is Earl of Althorp. Designed for lavish entertaining, Spencer House is a magnificent example of neo-classical interiors and furniture. By far the most impressive is the Great Room, which acted as a picture gallery, ballroom and reception room and includes a curved painted ceiling. Guided tours of the eight state rooms on the ground floor, including the Library, Dining Room, Painted Room and stunning green and gilded Palm room are available. Booking is recommended.

Opening hours
Sunday only 10am – 4.30pm

Nearest Underground
Green Park 5 minutes

www.spencerhouse.co.uk

Westminster Abbey

20 Dean's Yard, SW1P 3PA

Westminster Abbey's royal connections go back over 1,000 years and it has hosted coronations, weddings, funerals and countless royal events.

Since 1066, all British monarchs have been crowned at Westminster Abbey.

Queen Elizabeth II was crowned here in 1953, and King Charles III in 2023. Westminster Abbey is the location of the official St Edward's Chair (Coronation Chair) on which the new monarch sits to receive the Crown.

In 2011, Kate & William, The Prince & Princess of Wales were married here in a lavish ceremony watched around the world. Princess Anne, the Princess Royal, was married at the Abbey as did the Queen Mother. A total of sixteen royal weddings have been held here.

It was the venue for Harry and Meghan's last official event as senior royals, when they attended the annual Commonwealth Day service in March 2020.

At the front of the church is the Grave of the Unknown Soldier on which the bouquets carried by royal brides are traditionally placed the day after their wedding. Both Kate and Meghan's bouquets were placed here.

Among the many royal funerals held at the Abbey were those of Queen Elizabeth the Queen Mother in April 2002 and Diana, Princess of Wales in September 1997. In September 2022, the coffin of Queen Elisabeth II was brought here from Westminster Hall, borne on a gun carriage pulled by Royal Naval sailors. After the funeral ceremony, there was a final procession through London en route to Windsor Castle

Westminster Abbey where the Prince & Princess of Wales were married, where kings and queens are crowned, and Queen Elizabeth II funeral's was held.

where she was buried in St George's Chapel.

Westminster Abbey is regularly used for royal events like Queen Elizabeth's Silver, Gold and Diamond Jubilees, as well as special commemorative services such as VE Day and the 2018 service for victims of the London terror attack. Each year, it hosts the Westminster Field of Remembrance containing poppy bedecked crosses representing members of the armed services who had died in service. Members of the Royal Family come to place crosses in the Field of Remembrance during a special service. Harry and Meghan, Duke and Duchess of Suffolk, attended the opening of the Field of Remembrance in 2019, and the Prince & Princess of Wales the previous year.

In 2018, Queen Elizabeth II opened the Queen's Jubilee Gallery within the Abbey. Located in the medieval Triforium in the upper part of the church, it offers brilliant views down the Abbey Nave. On display in the Queen's Jubilee Gallery are over 300 items from the Abbey collection, including the marriage licence of the Prince & Princess of Wales, the fourteenth century Libera Regalis, which is the basis for all royal coronations and funerals held at the Abbey, as well as royal effigies and the oldest medieval altarpiece in the country.

Westminster Abbey has a very special royal status. It is known as Royal Peculiar because it belongs directly to the monarch, and is not controlled by a bishop of the Church of England. Instead, the Dean of Westminster reports directly to the King. It is also known as the Collegiate Church of St Peter, Westminster. Founded by Edward the Confessor in the eleventh century, it has always enjoyed close links with the monarchy. King Edward the Confessor, Mary Queen of Scots, Elizabeth I and Mary I are among the many kings and queens to be buried here.

Entry charge

Open daily, but times vary depending on whether there is a royal event or service taking place.

Nearest Underground
Westminster 5 minutes walk

www.westminster-abbey.org

Westminster Cathedral

Victoria Street, SW1P 1QW

Founded in 1895, Westminster Cathedral is the largest Roman Catholic cathedral in the UK and is the seat of the Roman Catholic Archbishop of Westminster. Queen Elizabeth II visited the Cathedral as part of her Silver Jubilee celebrations in 1977 in order to view a flower show. In 1995, she attended Choral Vespers as part of the Cathedral's centenary celebrations. This was the first time since the sixteenth century that a UK sovereign had attended such a service within a UK Roman Catholic church.

The Cathedral is quite a stunning building, distinctively constructed in horizontal stripes of brick and stone. It contains some stunning mosaics and art work, including intricate designs on the ceiling. Visitors who climb up to the Viewing Gallery (210 feet above street level) can enjoy spectacular views across Westminster. Also worth seeing is the Cathedral Treasures Exhibition containing rare ecclesiastical objects, relics, chalices, vestments plus a detailed model of the cathedral showing how it was designed and built.

Free entry

Opening hours
Monday to Friday 9.30 – 5pm
Weekends 9.30am – 6pm
Nearest Underground and Mainline
    Train: Victoria 5 minutes

www.westminstercathedral.org.uk

Westminster Cathedral is the largest Roman Catholic cathedral in the country, and has been visited by HM The Queen.

WEST END

Actors' Church

St Paul's Church, Bedford Street, Covent Garden, WC2E 9ED

Built by architect Inigo Jones in 1633, Covent Garden's parish church has become better known as the Actors' Church due to its long association with the theatre community and the sheer number of actor memorials inside.

Head for the south side of the church to enjoy the Diamond Jubilee Garden created in honour of Queen Elizabeth II. The Duchess of Gloucester opened it in 2013, on behalf of the Queen. At the centre of the maze is a reproduction of Queen Elizabeth's head as seen on the 1953 one penny coin. Until 1852, this area was the church burial ground and it includes the graves of victims of the Great Plague of London.

The Grand Portico at the front of the church is actually a fake doorway, but it has become extremely famous for its role in the opening scene of George Bernard Shaw's *Pygmalion* and Lerner and Lowe's *My Fair Lady*. A memorial on the south wall commemorates Queen Elizabeth II's visit in February 1988.

Admission free

Opening hours
Monday to Friday 8.30am – 5.30pm
Saturday opening dependent on
    events
Sunday 9am – 1pm

Nearest Underground
Covent Garden 5 minutes

www.actorschurch.org

Ainsworths

32 – 34 New Cavendish Street, W1G 8UF

Specialists in traditional homeopathic remedies and Bach Flower Remedies, Ainsworths held royal warrants from Queen Elisabeth II and the Prince of Wales. Their pharmacy and consulting rooms in New Cavendish Street offer a range of over 4,200 remedies, with a team of homeopaths available to provide help and advice.

Opening hours
Monday to Friday 9am – 6pm
Saturday 9am – 4pm

Nearest Underground
Bond Street 8 minutes

www.ainsworths.com

Albert Amor

37 Bury Street, St James, SW1Y 6AU

Dealers for over 100 years in English porcelain, they held a royal warrant from Queen Elizabeth II. The company holds themed selling exhibitions in spring and autumn.

Albert Amor was first appointed Antiquary to Queen Mary with the duty of seeking suitable items for the Royal Collection. Not all the items suggested were accepted, as a note in the company's archives reveal. Her lady in waiting, the Marchioness of Cambridge wrote that Queen Mary doesn't want these coasters, but I do!

Nearest Underground
Green Park 6 minutes
Piccadilly circus 8 minutes

www.albertamor.co.uk

Arnold Wiggins & Sons Ltd

31 Bury Street, St James, SW1Y 6AU

The company were picture framers to Queen Elizabeth II. Arnold Wiggins provides antique and reproduction frames for Old Master and modern paintings plus works on paper, together with framing advice. They work extensively with museums and collectors, sourcing originals and making reproduction frames as needed.

Nearest Underground
Green Park 6 minutes
Piccadilly Circus 8 minutes

Asprey

167 New Bond Street, W1S 4AY

Founded in 1781, this is a luxury emporium par excellence and has supplied crowns, coronets and sceptres for royal families worldwide. It was granted its first royal warrant by Queen Victoria, and held one for Prince Charles, Prince of Wales.

In 1953, Asprey created a Coronation Year Gold Collection in 18 carat gold featuring a dessert, coffee and liqueur service which went on show instore, and later toured the US. More recently, it designed the Heart of the Ocean necklace featured in James Cameron's film, *Titanic*.

The New Bond Street store is one of the largest Asprey stores worldwide. A glass room atrium connects various historic buildings. Jewellery, crystal, silver, china and leather goods are displayed in store.

Opening hours
Monday to Saturday 10am – 6pm

www.asprey.com

Bellamy's Restaurant

Bruton Place, W1J 6LY

A fine dining French brasserie-style restaurant, Bellamy's was a favourite dining location of Queen Elizabeth II. She celebrated her eightieth birthday here and attended various private dinners here, including one with the Princess Royal.

Established in 2004, Bellamy's is an oyster and sandwich bar at lunchtime. In the evening it transforms into an elegant cocktail bar and restaurant. Menu staples include Iced Lobster soufflé, Smoked Eel Mousse, Fillet of Dover sole, Whitebait with cheese croquettes and crab salad, and Marina's Chocolate cake.

Nearest Underground
Green Park 3 minutes walk
Bond Street 5 minutes walk

www.bellamysrestaurant.co.uk

Bentley & Skinner

55 Piccadilly, W1J 0DX

Bentley & Skinner are a British company specialising in fine antique jewellery and *objet d'art* by Carl Fabergé. They have been supplying jewellery to the Royal Family since the reign of Queen Victoria. They held royal warrants as jewellers and silversmiths to Queen Elizabeth II and Prince Charles, Prince of Wales.

Opening hours
Monday to Saturday 10am – 5.30pm

Nearest Underground
Piccadilly 6 minutes

www.bentley-skinner.co.uk

Berry Bros. & Rudd

3 St James's Street, SW1Y 5HZ

In 1688, Berry Bros. & Rudd began trading as wine merchants at 3 St James's Street. Since the reign of King George III, they have been an official wine supplier to the Royal Family. The company held royal warrants from Queen Elizabeth II and Prince Charles.

The St James's street outlet has changed little since it was first opened, with the historic cellars and townhouse acting as a venue for wine schools, wine tasting and bespoke events. Shop trading now takes place just round the corner at 63 Pall Mall. This is where you can choose from over 1,300 different wines and spirits from all over the world, at prices ranging from £10 to £10,000 per bottle.

Berry Bros. & Rudd is still a family business, run by the eighth generation of the family.

A blocked underground tunnel leads directly from their cellars to St James's Palace, which would certainly have made supplying the royal court quite easy!

Opening hours
Monday to Friday 10am – 7pm
Saturday 10am – 5pm

Nearest Underground
Green Park 7 minutes
Piccadilly Circus 9 minutes

www.bbr.com

Bocca di Lupo

Archer Street, Soho, W1D 7BB

An Italian restaurant in the heart of London's theatreland, Bocca di Lupo specialises in regional food, particularly for lunch and theatre specials. It was a favourite of the Duchess of Sussex during her time in the UK. Apart from the restaurant, it has a fantastic Gelateria selling Italian style ice cream, freshly made each day. The hardest part is choosing from the extensive range of available flavours. Apart from the usual ones like Strawberry and Vanilla, you can expect unusual ones like Bonet (chocolate, rum, amaretti biscuits and coffee) or Gorgonzola, Dates and Walnut.

Nearest Underground

Piccadilly Circus 3 minutes
Dean Street 4 minutes

www.boccadilupo.com

British Museum

Great Russell Street, Bloomsbury, WC1B 3DG

Founded in 1753, the British Museum is the world's oldest national public museum. It opened to the public in 1759 with the aim of being free to 'studious and curious persons'. This is a 'must see' museum for any visitor to London due to the sheer extent of items on display. Whatever your interest, you are guaranteed that there will be something to amaze within the sixty massive, labyrinthine galleries. There are treasures to be seen from all over the world, including Egyptian

The British Museum is the world's oldest national public museum.

mummies, Greek and Roman objects, and items from Mexico, India, China and South Asia, Medieval Europe, Americas and the Islamic World. Among the more unusual items on display are Sutton Hoo Anglo Saxon treasures, intricate clocks and watches, the Lewis Chessmen, drawings by Raphael and a replica traditional Japanese tea house.

Queen Elizabeth II visited the British Museum many times, such as in 2017 when she toured the refurbished Sir Joseph Hotung Gallery of China and South Asia – twenty-five years after she first opened it! Other major exhibitions here that attracted the Queen's interest included the Treasures of Tutankhamun in 1972, and the Gilded Dragon exhibition in 1999 when she accompanied the Chinese President Jiang Zemin who was in the UK on a state visit. In 2000, Queen Elizabeth II opened the Great Court commenting that 'the British Museum is a remarkable phenomenon.'
Various guided tours and talks take place daily – ask at the Hands On desk in the Great Court for more information.

Free entry, but tickets must be purchased for special exhibitions.

Open daily
Great Court 9am – 6pm
Galleries 10am – 5.30 pm
Closed Christmas and New Year's Day

Nearest Underground
Tottenham Court Road 5 minutes
Holborn 7 minutes
Russell Square 7 minutes

www.britishmuseum.org

Burberry
121 Regent Street, W1B 4TB

An iconic British company, Burberry held royal warrants from Queen Elizabeth II and Prince Charles, Prince of Wales. Founded by Thomas Burberry over a hundred years ago, the company is renowned for its rainwear and coats. Burberry invented Gabardine fabric, designed to be breathable, waterproof and hard wearing, which was used in garments worn by Ernest Shackleton during his Antarctic expeditions. The company also created trench coats, and its Burberry check design is now registered as a trademark. The distinctive Prince of Wales check is one of their most popular designs.

Members of the Royal Family are often seen wearing Burberry items. On arrival at Kings Lynn station in Norfolk *en route* to Sandringham, Queen Elizabeth II wore a Burberry headscarf. The Princess of Wales wore a Burberry shirt while visiting Yellowknife, Canada, a trench coat during a visit to Belfast and a Burberry coat when visiting Stockholm. Meghan, Duchess of Sussex was photographed in a Burberry trench coat while touring New Zealand just after her pregnancy had been announced, and wore a Burberry double-breasted tartan coat for her first visit to Edinburgh with Prince Harry in 2018.

Opening hours
Monday to Saturday 10am – 8pm
Sunday 11.30am – 6pm

Nearest Underground
Piccadilly Circus 5 minutes
Oxford Circus 8 minutes

www.burberry.com

Cartier

40 – 41 Old Bond Street, W1S 4QR
175 – 177 New Bond Street, W1S 4RL

Edward VII claimed Cartier was 'jeweller of kings and the king of jewellers'. He ordered twenty-seven tiaras for use at his coronation, and the royal link has been continuously maintained. The Duke of Windsor ordered an iconic Flamingo brooch for Wallis Simpson. Princess Diana received a yellow gold Patek Philippe watch as a twentieth birthday present from Prince Charles. In later years she added two versions of the Tank wristwatch – a Tank Louis Cartier and a Tank Française, which was a gift from her father. Following her death, Prince William chose the Tank Française as a keepsake.

Kate Middleton wore a diamond and platinum Cartier tiara known as the Halo Tiara for her wedding to Prince William. Cartier had originally created this tiara for Queen Elizabeth the Queen Mother, then Duchess of York in 1936. Kate is often seen wearing a Cartier Balloon Bleu Watch, which she acquired in 2014.

Meghan Markle is a fan of Cartier. At her wedding she wore Cartier Reflection de Cartier earrings and bracelet, and Cartier Studs when attending Prince Louis' christening. On her first outing after her marriage to Prince Harry, she wore a Cartier tennis bracelet (a gift from her new husband) to King Charles' seventieth birthday celebrations.

The New Bond Street store is one of Cartier's three flagship stores worldwide. It is also one of their biggest, stocking an extensive range of items. Just round the corner is the Old Bond Street store, complete with chandeliers and walls lined with lemon yellow leather.

Opening hours
Monday to Saturday 10am – 6pm
Closed Sundays

Nearest Underground
Bond Street 5 minutes to New Bond Street
10 minutes to Old Bond street store

www.cartier.com

Charbonnel et Walker

Bond Street, Mayfair, W1S 4BT

The home of irresistibly luscious chocolate since its creation back in 1875 when Edward VII (then Prince of

Wales) encouraged Mrs Walker and Mme Charbonnel to open a store in Bond Street. Royal links have continued, and Charbonnel et Walker held a royal warrant as chocolate makers to Queen Elizabeth II. In the *Wonderful World of Chocolate* documentary on Channel 5 in 2020, a look behind the scenes at Charbonnel revealed that the Queen had a fondness for floral chocolates, especially Rose and Violet creams. Other Royal fans have included Princess Diana and Princess Margaret. Princess Diana used to buy Charbonnel et Walker Easter eggs for her two sons.

All the chocolates are made to traditional recipes handed down over the decades. Dark chocolate and truffles are especially popular. Wandering into the elegant Bond Street Store within the Royal Arcade is a mouth-watering experience, with rows of delicious chocolates laid out on counters, waiting for your personal selection. Alternatively there are numerous gift boxes, hampers, chocolate bars and sugar confectionary already prepared for purchase.

Opening hours
Monday to Saturday 10am – 6pm
Sunday 12 noon – 5pm

Nearest Underground
Bond Street 10 minutes

www.charbonnel.co.uk

Chiltern Firehouse

1 Chiltern Street, Mayfair, W1U 7PA

Princess Beatrice and Princess Eugenie are often seen here. It was the venue for Princess Beatrice's engagement party. Meghan, Duchess of Suffolk was seen sipping cocktails at the Chiltern Firehouse before she and Prince Harry moved to California.

The Firehouse is well-known for its brunches and stylish contemporary food based on seasonality and healthy eating. Typical cocktails include Mary Celeste (Tanqueray Ten Gin, Mignotte and Oyster) and New York Classic (Ketel One Vodka, spice mix and lemon).

Nearest Underground
Portman Square 4 minutes

www.chilternfirehouse.com

Claridge's Hotel

Brook Street, Mayfair, W1K 4HR

An iconic five-star luxury London hotel regarded as the epitome of pure elegance, an Art Deco paradise and described as an 'annex to Buckingham Palace' due to the number of heads of state have stayed here during official visits. During the London Olympics, one caller apparently phoned the hotel asking to be put through to the president – the operator answered quite simply: 'Which one?' During the Second World War, it became the home of the kings of Greece, Norway and Yugoslavia.

An iconic hotel often regarded as an 'annex to Buckingham Palace'.

One of the suites – 212 – was even temporarily declared to be Yugoslavian territory so that Crown Prince Alexander could be born in Yugoslavia. It has remained a popular destination with European royalty as well as the UK Royal Family. During state visits, many heads of state choose Claridge's as the venue for return state dinners for the King.

Queen Elizabeth II attended numerous banquets at Claridge's, as well as various private occasions. Queen Elizabeth, the Queen Mother used to have a favourite table in the restaurant, which was always adorned with sweet peas. The Prince & Princess of Wales attended an official function with the Thirty Club at Claridge's.

David Linley, the Queen's nephew, designed twenty-five Linley Suites for Claridge's. The Royal Suite reopened in 2020, adorned with bespoke silk de Gournay wallpaper and furnished with chairs in Buckingham-blue silk with glistening golden thread made by the royal weavers, Gainsborough.

The opulent lobby at Claridge's Hotel.

The hotel is renowned for its discretion and rarely talks about royals staying in its Royal Suite.

Nearest Underground
Bond Street 5 minutes

www.claridges.co.uk

Covent Garden

Traditionally a fruit and vegetable market, this area has become very much a centre for entertainment and transport. Royal connections go back a long way, with Charles II's most notorious mistress Nell Gwynne selling fruit in the market before gaining fame as an actress in Drury Lane. Modern royals can often be found attending performances at theatres in the area, especially the Royal Opera House.

If you love opera and ballet, this is definitely the theatre for you as this is the home of both the Royal Ballet Company and the Royal Opera Company. Queen Elizabeth II was patron of both organisations. It is one of the oldest working theatres in London, as there has been a theatre on the site since 1732. Members of the Royal Family frequently attend gala performances at the Royal Opera House. The Princess of Wales has made several visits to the theatre. In 2017, she made a surprise visit to see The Nutcracker, while in 2018 she arrived with Princess Charlotte to watch a dress rehearsal of The Nutcracker. The following year, she visited the Royal Opera House to discover more about the work of the costume department, their use of textiles and to talk to dancers of the Royal Ballet.

Princess Diana also loved ballet, frequently attending performances at the Royal Opera House where she struck up a close friendship with dancer Wayne Sleep. She even

Members of the Royal Family frequently attend performances at Covent Garden's Royal Opera House.

performed on its stage during a memorable event in 1985. During a private show for supporters of the Royal Opera House, Diana appeared on stage dancing with Wayne Sleep to the music of Uptown Girl by Billy Joel, as a surprise for her husband, Prince Charles, who was in the audience.

Apart from booking seats to watch performances within the stunning auditorium, you can book guided tours of the Royal Opera House. A variety of tours are available including a backstage and front of house tour to see how the theatre prepares for an evening performance, tours focusing on the history and operation of the theatre, and following in the footsteps of performers entering via the stage door. One of the more unusual tours is the Velvet, Gilt and Glamour tour. This is a special tour of the auditorium focusing on the architecture, as well visiting the royal retiring rooms still used by royalty today. All these tours must be pre-booked.

Nearest Underground
Covent Garden 1 minute

www.roh.org.uk

Daks Simpson

10 Old Bond Street, W1S 4PL

Daks Simpson were outfitters to Queen Elizabeth II and the Duke of Edinburgh. The brand is also popular with King Charles III. A quintessential classic fashion luxury brand offering fine tailoring and accessories, it has a flagship store on Old Bond Street. Founded by Simeon Simpson in 1894, the original department store traded as Simpsons of Piccadilly and inspired the popular TV sitcom *Are You Being Served?* A former employee recalled visits to the store by the Duke of Edinburgh in the 1940s.

Opening hours
Monday to Wednesday, Friday, Saturday
   10am – 6.30pm
Thursday 10am – 6.30pm
Sunday 12.00 – 6pm

Nearest Underground
Piccadilly Circus 7 minutes
Bond Street 10 minutes

www.daks.com

Dean Street Townhouse

Dean Street, Soho, W1D 3SE

It was in a quiet corner of the Dean Street Townhouse that Prince Harry had a blind date with Meghan Markle. Apparently it is one of her favourite hotels. He commented 'I was beautifully surprised when I walked into that room and saw her.' Since then they returned on at least one other occasion. A thirty-nine bedroom hotel and restaurant located in elegant Georgian buildings, it offers brunch, afternoon tea and a late night menu as well as modern British seasonal food served all day long. It is a great place to relax with a classy cocktail or two, especially if you like

modern art, since the walls are adorned with works by Tracey Emin, Keith Tyson and various emerging British artists. Pre-booking tables is recommended as it is very popular.

The site has other notable royal connections. Before this Georgian townhouse was built, it was the site of a house here belonging to Charles II's famous mistress, Nell Gwynne, in which she made her home for many years. During the 1920s and 1930s, various royal princes often came to the house as it was a popular entertainment club attracting people like Noël Coward and Fred Astaire.

Opening hours
Monday to Thursday 7am – midnight
Friday 7am – 1am
Saturday 8am – 1am
Sunday 8am – 11pm

Nearest Underground
Dean Street 4 minutes
Tottenham Court Road 6 minutes

www.deanstreettownhouse.com

Dorchester Hotel

Park Lane, Mayfair, W1K 1QA

With views across to Hyde Park, the Dorchester is one of the most luxurious five-star hotels in London. Its concierge service promises the ultimate 'gold standard of care' when it comes to satisfying any requests. You can even use their fleet of iconic classic cars for transfers, sightseeing trips or making a grand entrance at special events.

Queen Elizabeth II was a regular visitor to the Dorchester, and was here on the night of 9 July 1947 just before her engagement to Prince Philip was announced. In 1990, Prince Philip unveiled a plaque in the hotel lobby marking the hotel's reopening following an extensive refurbishment.

Afternoon tea at the Dorchester is one of its specialities, full of tradition and a tremendous amount of cake! One of its more unusual services includes masterclasses with The Dorchester's executive chef. It is quite an experience since it includes a private breakfast, masterclass, champagne reception and finally lunch at the Chef's Table.

The Dorchester was the first hotel worldwide to be built from reinforced concrete. During the Second World War, it was home to General Eisenhower, Supreme Commander of the Allied Forces in Europe, while planning D-Day and the invasion of Normandy. The Eisenhower Suite is named in his honour, and contains a variety of historical memorabilia.

Nearest Underground
Hyde Park Corner 5 minutes

www.dorchestercollection.com

Floris
89 Jermyn Street, SW1Y 6JH

Floris supplied perfumes to Queen Elizabeth II, and toilet preparations to Prince Charles when he was Prince of Wales. Since their foundation in 1730,

the company has held nineteen royal warrants. Their first royal involvement was in 1820 when Floris were appointed Smooth Pointed Comb Maker to King George IV. Princess Diana opened the Floris factory in Devon in 1989. The company remains still a family owned business, run by the ninth generation.

In 2013, Floris created a very special fragrance in honour of the Queen's Diamond Jubilee: Royal Arms Diamond Edition. This was an updated version

The Floris sign complete with the Royal Arms adorning the outside of the store.

of Royal Arms created to celebrate the Queen's birth in 1926. Floris crafted a limited edition of this special fragrance, using antique crystal bottles that had been discovered wrapped in newspaper within the Floris warehouse. One of those unique bottles was displayed at the Queen's July 2013 Coronation Festival within the gardens of Buckingham Palace.

Floris have created various bespoke fragrances for the royal family, including a unisex fragrance made available to celebrate the wedding of the Duke and Duchess of Sussex in 2018.

The Jermyn Street store contains a museum gallery complete with original mahogany cabinets and glasswork purchased at the 1851 Great Exhibition. Visitors can see various archive items, including fragrances from customer ledges dating back centuries. There have been many famous customers, including Sir Winston Churchill, Marilyn Monroe (wore Rose Geranium), Benedict Cumberbatch and Liv Tyler. Florence Nightingale wrote thanking Mr Floris for his 'beautiful sweet-smelling nosegays' while in *Diamonds Are Forever*, 007 states he 'would have to send a cable to May to get things fixed. Let's see – flowers, bath essence from Floris, air the sheets.'

Customers can buy perfumes in store, or book a customisation service to tailor perfume to suit their personality.

Opening hours

Monday to Wednesday, Friday, Saturday
   9.30am – 6.30pm
Thursday 9.30am – 7pm
Sunday 11.30am – 5.30pm

Nearest Underground

Piccadilly Circus 4 minutes
Green Park 7 minutes

www.florislondon.com

Fortnum & Mason

181 Piccadilly, W1A 1ER

Founded in 1707 by Hugh Mason and William Fortnum, it has steadily developed into one of the premier grocery stores in London and even invented the Scotch Egg! Nowadays it is better known as an iconic brand providing high quality teas, coffee and food.

The company has been supplying royalty for over 150 years. In 1856, Queen Victoria ordered Fortnum's to 'dispatch without delay to Miss Nightingale in Scutari, a huge consignment of concentrated beef tea.' In 1902, King Edward VII gave it a further challenge asking it to 'Bring me the finest tea in all the land.' Staff from Fortnum & Mason promptly travelled the world to bring back the best teas they could find: Assam from India, and Flowery Pekoe from Sri Lanka. A blend of the two teas resulted in a smooth honey like tea which is still in use under the Royal Blend brand name. Fortnum & Mason held royal warrants as suppliers

Fortnum & Mason, the luxury grocers on Piccadilly which has been supplying royalty for over 150 years.

Inside Fortnums, Paddington Bear guards the provisions.

to Queen Elizabeth II and King Charles, when he was Prince of Wales.

Head in store for an irresistible choice of wine and spirits, chocolate, biscuits and exclusive loose leaf teas, including many rare varieties. There is also an extensive food hall, ice cream parlour and several restaurants. Meghan Markle is said to have given her friend Daniel Martin chocolate truffles from Fortnum & Mason when he visited her at Kensington Palace.

Opening hours
10am – 8pm daily
12 noon – 6pm Sunday

Nearest Underground
Piccadilly Circus 2 minutes

www.fortnumandmason.com

Hauser & Wirth

23 Savile Row, Mayfair, W1S 2ET

Princess Eugenie has worked here for several years. Hauser & Wirth specialises in contemporary and modern art from around the world involving both emerging and established artists. It has branches in Zurich, New York and Hong Kong in addition to London.

The London branch has two exhibition spaces, north and south. It organises a range of events throughout the year including artist talks, film screenings, workshops and exhibitions. There is a gallery shop containing items crafted by international and local makers, artist collaborations and a range of books published by Hauser & Wirth.

Typical exhibitions held at Hauser & Wirth have included Isa Genzken's Window, focusing on travel themes through the medium of an aircraft cabin; and Mark Bradford's Cerberus, based on ancient mythology.

Nearest Underground
Oxford Circus 6 minutes

www.hauserwirth.com

Hatchards

187 Piccadilly, W1J 9LE

Believed to be the oldest bookshop in the UK, Hatchards opened a store on Piccadilly in 1797. It has been in the same location since 1810. It held royal warrants from Queen Elizabeth II, The Duke of Edinburgh and King Charles when he was Prince of Wales.

The five-storey building contains a comprehensive book range covering all possible subjects, as well as offering a regular programme of events, customer evenings, book signings and a subscription service.

Opening hours
Monday to Saturday 9.30am – 8pm
Sunday 12 noon – 6.30pm

Nearest Underground
Piccadilly Circus 4 minutes
Green Park 5 minutes

www.hatchards.co.uk

Heywood Hill

10 Curzon Street, W1J 5HH

A small bookshop occupying two floors of a Georgian townhouse, it has even been mentioned in John Le Carré's *Tinker Tailor Soldier Spy* novel. Heywood Hill held a royal warrant to supply books to Queen Elizabeth II.

Don't expect to find modern blockbusters here. Instead the focus is on new, second-hand, antiquarian fiction and non-fiction, especially history, architecture, biography, travel, sport and children's books. Heywood Hill is owned by the Duke of Devonshire, and his aunt, the famous writer Nancy Mitford, worked there during the Second World War. She forgot to lock up one evening and next morning arrived to find the shop 'full of wandering people trying to buy books from each other.' Customer service is a priority, curating libraries for customers and hotels as well as providing a monthly selection of titles for over 700 customers worldwide based on discussions about which authors and genre they love or hate.

Opening hours
Monday to Friday 9.30am – 6pm
Closed weekends

Nearest Underground
Green Park 4 minutes
Bond Street 12 minutes

www.heywoodhill.com

House Of Garrard

24 Albemarle Street, Mayfair, W1S 4HT

Royal connections go back a long way. Garrard is the longest serving jeweller in the world, dating back to 1735 when it received a royal commission from Frederick, Prince of Wales (eldest son of George II). Since then it has served every British monarch, making numerous famous items, including Queen Mary's consort crown in 1911. When Queen Elizabeth II married Prince Philip, her veil was held in place by a

House of Garrard – the longest serving royal jeweller in the world.

Garrard creation, a beautiful fringed tiara originally made for Queen Mary in 1919.

By far the most famous modern royal piece of jewellery has to be the spectacular sapphire and diamond ring given by Prince Charles to Diana Spencer in 1981. Many years later, Prince William gave it to his bride to be, Kate Middleton, who now wears it constantly.

Garrard have designed medals granted by the Queen such as the DSO and CBE. Prince Harry commissioned them to devise gold, silver and bronze participant medals for the Invictus Games.

They have also made many presentation pieces such as the Royal Ascot Gold Cup and the Premier League football trophy.

Their exquisite jewellery is characterised by a desire to bring out the natural beauty of precious stones, while achieving a balance between tradition and design.

Garrard held a royal warrant from King Charles, when he was Prince of Wales.

Opening hours
Weekdays 10am – 6pm
Sunday 10am – 5pm

Nearest Underground
Bond Street 10 minutes
Green Park 5 minutes

www.garrard.com

The luxurious boutique interior at the House of Garrard.

The Ivy

West Street, WC2H 9NQ

Founded in 1917, The Ivy Restaurant has long been a popular destination with members of the Royal Family seeking an intimate place for dinner. Queen Elizabeth was one of many royals who have dined at The Ivy for example in 2017 when she visited for a friend's private celebration.

The Ivy specialises in classic and modern contemporary British dishes. An elegant restaurant, the sumptuous décor includes many contemporary art works. Among the notable features of the restaurant are the Art Deco harlequin pattern stained glass windows.

Nearest Underground
Leicester Square 3 minutes
Covent Garden 4 minutes

www.the-ivy.co.uk

John Lobb Bootmakers

9 St James's Street, SW1A 1EF

Esquire magazine describe the John Lobb store in St James 'the most beautiful shop in the world'. Located close to the gate tower of St James, it is an elegantly wood-panelled store selling exclusive bespoke shoes and accessories. Founded in 1849 by John Lobb, their quality footwear was noticed by the Palace. The company was awarded a royal warrant as bootmaker to Edward Prince of Wales, later King Edward VII, and held a warrant from the Duke of Edinburgh, as well as King Charles, when he was Prince of Wales. Still a family business, they can take up to seven months to produce bespoke hand-made shoes, allowing time for fitting, creating moulds and manufacture. Other famous clients have included Frank Sinatra, Dean Martin, Roald Dahl, George Bernard Shaw and Lord Olivier. Hermes of Paris are licenced to manufacture a range of ready to wear shoes under the John Lobb brand.

Nearest Underground
Piccadilly Circus 2 minutes

www.johnlobbltd.co.uk

Justerini & Brooks

61 St James's Street, SW1A 1LZ

Established in 1749, Justerini & Brooks have supplied every reigning monarch since King George III's coronation in 1761. Princess Diana and her father, Earl Spencer, were regular clients. In 1997, the Queen Mother granted the company a royal warrant. During her 100th birthday celebrations, she attended a lunch in her honour in the company's private dining room.

Justerini & Brooks sells fine wines to private collectors around the world, and has an extensive online business.

Nearest Underground
Piccadilly Circus 2 minutes

www.justerinis.com

Leicester Square Odeon Luxe Cinema

Leicester Square, WC2H 7LQ

Glittering, glamorous Royal Command Performances attract massive crowds both outside and in – which means only the biggest cinema will serve. Leicester Square Odeon Luxe is that venue. The very first Royal Command Performance took place in 1946 at what was then the Empire Cinema, and was attended by King George VI and Queen Elizabeth together with Princess Elizabeth and Princess Margaret. The chosen film was *A Matter of Life and Death*. Since then there have been over seventy Royal Command charity performances at Leicester Square including *To Catch A Thief*, *Close Encounters of the Third Kind*, *Passage to India*, *Titanic* and *Spectre*. Queen Elizabeth II attended numerous productions here. The King and Queen Consort Camilla attended a Royal Film Premiere of Sam Mendes' highly evocative film entitled *1917* while the Prince & Princess of Wales attended the UK premier of Top Gun at Leicester Square.

Quite apart from Royal Film Performances, this Leicester Square venue is also used for global and European film premieres, often attended by members of the Royal Family. Originally built in 1937, the Art Deco auditorium is beautifully decorated. Throughout the year, there is a continuous programme of concerts and films available.

Nearest Underground
Leicester Square 1 minute

www.odeon.co.uk/london_
leicestersquare

Liberty Of London

Regent Street, W1B 5AH

Royal style icon, the Princess of Wales, is often seen wearing Liberty print dresses such as the pretty green and brown paisley print Ridley London's Virginia silk chiffon dress she wore while visiting Warren Park in June 2019. Princess Charlotte has been pictured several times in Liberty print smock dresses, just like her grandmother Queen Elizabeth II when she was a child.

These designs are unique to Liberty of London, and form part of its extensive fabric archives.

The distinctive mock Tudor black and white store has been an important part of the Regent Street shopping experience since 1875. Founded by Arthur Lasenby Liberty, it began by selling ornaments, fabric and *objet d'art* from Japan and the Far East. It quickly became the most fashionable place to shop in London, and began creating its own designs, many of which were commissioned from the Pre-Raphaelite artist, William Morris.

It is still the place to go for high quality fabrics, clothing, high-end fashion, soft furnishings, wallpaper and accessories. Floral and graphic prints are a speciality.

Opening hours
Monday to Saturday 10am – 9pm
Sunday 11.30am – 6pm
Public holidays 12 noon – 6pm

Nearest Underground
Oxford Street 2 minutes
Piccadilly Circus 9 minutes

www.libertylondon.com

London Palladium

Argyll Street, Soho, W1F 7TF

The London Palladium is one of the best-known theatres in London having hosted the annual Royal Variety Performance forty-three times – more than any other theatre. Acts vary from year to year and have included The Beatles, Diversity, comedians, magicians and dance groups. A member of the Royal Family is always in attendance at this performance as it is a major fundraising event for the Royal Variety charity of which Queen Elizabeth II was patron. Queen Elizabeth attended in 2012, and the Prince & Princess of Wales attended in 2014, 2017 and 2019. The Duke of Sussex attended in 2015, and was accompanied by Meghan Markle in 2018.

Apart from the Royal Variety Show, the London Palladium hosted the Royal Birthday Gala in honour of Queen Elizabeth the Queen Mother's ninetieth birthday. Other famous productions include *The Wizard of Oz*, *Chitty Chitty*

Bang Bang, *Dick Whittington*, *Eugenius*, *Sister Act* and *Madonna's* Madam X tour.

Surprisingly, the Royal Box does not offer the best view of the stage as it is sited to one side of the theatre. Members of the Royal Family wanting to see a show rather than attend a gala or special event, simply book tickets like anyone else!

Pre-booked backstage tours are held from time to time, taking visitors around the theatre, front and back of house, as well as going on the stage itself. It is a great way to discover the history of this historic theatre, which opened in 1910 as a Palace of Varieties. Such tours must be pre-booked.

Pre-book performance tickets if you want a specific date, although some may be available on the door.

www.backstagetheatretours.com

London Transport Museum

Covent Garden, WC2E 7BB

Ever wondered what it was like to travel on the underground in days gone by? This is where you can find out – just as King Charles and Queen Consort Camilla discovered in early 2020. Their visit was certainly memorable as a special eco-friendly red double decker bus collected them from their home at Clarence House to take them to the Museum – along with a group of school children. During the visit, they sat in a 1939 underground carriage, while the Queen Consort tried out a one person air raid shelter

The London Transport Museum in Covent Garden.

commenting ironically 'I am self-isolating'. Their visit marked the twentieth anniversary of Transport for London.

A very popular museum, it contains over 500,000 items relating to urban public transport, many of which date back to the 1920s and include a unique collection of poster art encouraging people to use public transport. It covers both the bus network and the underground. Among the vehicles on display are the locomotives that powered the world's first underground railway in the late nineteenth century, as well as iconic London red buses.

Entry charge

Opening hours
10am – 6 pm daily
Friday 11am – 6pm

Nearest Underground
Covent Garden 5 minutes

www.ltmuseum.co.uk

Mahiki Night Club

Dover Street, W1S 4LD

Mahiki has become the place to go if you want to enjoy Polynesian Tiki style entertainment. Rum is the main drink on offer. It's creative and fun with cocktails served in coconut shells and treasure chests. Some nights are specially themed such as Boho Beach on Tuesdays, and a Rum Cocktail Club on Fridays.

This is definitely a very exclusive and upmarket venue. It is very popular with celebrities like Madonna and Lady Gaga, together with younger royals including Princess Beatrice and Princess Eugenie. Over the years, there have been numerous stories in the media, including references to Prince Harry spilling champagne then licking it up!

Nearest Underground
Green Park 3 minutes

www.mahiki.co.uk

Molton Brown

227 Regent Street, Mayfair, W1B 2EF
Molton Brown supplied toiletries to Queen Elizabeth II. All the products on sale are carefully blended with 'a touch of London eccentricity for bold fragrances and bright colours'. The company's signature perfumes, bath and shower gels, home and hand care products are found in five-star hotels, luxury department stores and stylish homes around the world.

Opening hours
10am – 8pm daily
Sundays 6pm

Nearest Underground
Oxford Circus 2 minutes
Bond Street 7 minutes

www.moltonbrown.co.uk

National Gallery

Trafalgar Square, WC2N 5DN

King Charles III has been associated with the National Gallery for a long time. A keen artist himself, he was a trustee between 1986 – 1993 and became its first Royal Patron in 2016.

His involvement has not always been amicable. The National Gallery featured in one of one of his most controversial remarks about contemporary architecture. In 1984, while attending a gala evening marking the 150th anniversary of the Royal Institute of British Architects at Hampton Court Palace, he described the proposed National Gallery extension as 'a monstrous carbuncle on the face of a much-loved and elegant friend'. The planned design was eventually scrapped and replaced with a different style.

Founded in 1824, the National Gallery occupies a prominent place in Trafalgar Square. It owns a collection of over 2,300 paintings covering a period from the mid thirteenth century to 1900, and includes most major artistic developments in Western painting from Giotto to Cézanne. Among its most important masterpieces are Vermeer's *Young Woman standing at a Virginal*, Titian's *Bacchus and Ariadne*, Van Gogh's *Sunflowers*, Michelangelo's *Entombment*, *The Fighting Temeraire* by Turner, and *The Hay Wain* by John Constable. All the key European

The National Gallery in Trafalgar Square contains paintings from all major artistic styles from Giotto to Cézanne.

painters are represented here including Leonardo Da Vinci, Velazquez, Rubens, Rembrandt, Botticelli and Stubbs.

There is a regular programme of special exhibitions, often including works from other galleries worldwide. Typical topics include Titian: Love, Desire, Death, Paul Gaugin, Monet and Architecture.

Access to the galleries is free, but special exhibitions incur a charge.

Opening hours
10am – 6pm daily
Closed 1 January, 24, 25, 26 December

Nearest Underground
Charing Cross 2 minutes
Leicester Square 1 minute

www.nationalgallery.org.uk

National Portrait Gallery
St Martin's Place, WC2H 0HE

Located just around the corner from the National Gallery, the National Portrait Gallery contains the most extensive collection of portraits in the world. On display are numerous portraits of UK sovereigns, their consorts and families including the Royal Family centenary portrait. There are numerous photographic images of members of the Royal Family including childhood photos of Prince Charles and Princess Anne. Also on display are portraits of Prince William and Prince Harry, as well as the first official portrait created of the Princess of Wales soon after her wedding to Prince William. Painted by Paul Emsley, Kate's face emerges out of a dark background. It can be seen in the Lerner Gallery.

Opened in 1856, the National Portrait Gallery was the first such portrait gallery to be opened worldwide. It contains a vast array of portraits of royalty and historically important and famous British people.

The Princess of Wales is patron of the National Portrait Gallery, and she has attended numerous events such as the 2019 Portrait Gala.

Entry is free, but special exhibitions incur a charge

Opening hours
10am – 6pm daily
Closed 24 – 26 December

Nearest Underground
Charing Cross 2 minutes
Leicester Square 1 minute

www.npg.org.uk

Noël Coward Theatre

85 – 88 St Martin's Lane, Covent Garden, WC2N 4AP

Wearing a dark Eponine dress for the occasion, the Prince & Princess of Wales watched a performance of *Dear Evan Hansen* at the Noël Coward theatre in January 2020. It was a special charity performance in support of the Royal Foundation. Before the performance they chatted about mental health with the play's author and composers while standing in the foyer.

An Edwardian Grade II listed building, it has been renamed several times since it was constructed in 1903, and became the Noël Coward theatre in 2006.

Nearest Underground
Leicester Square 3 minutes

www.noelcowardtheatre.co.uk

Paxton & Whitfield

93 Jermyn Street, SW1Y 6JE

Cheesemonger to Queen Elizabeth II and King Charles III, Paxton & Whitfield is one of the oldest cheese merchants in the country. It has been sourcing and maturing cheeses for over 200 years and has served all the royal households since being appointed cheesemonger to Queen Victoria in 1850.

Sir Winston Churchill commented 'a gentleman only buys his cheese from Paxton & Whitfield.'

The Jermyn Street store is Paxton & Whitfield's original store, and still has a historic atmosphere with its distinctive black and gold shop front and interior décor. Many of the cheeses on display have been matured in the underground cellars below the store. It is a great place to buy cheese, wine biscuits, chutneys and preserves. Events are frequently held here including tutored tastings and cheese and wine matching.

Elegant exterior of one of the oldest cheese merchants in the country.

The perfect place to buy cheese and preserves.

Opening hours
Monday to Saturday 9.30am – 6pm

Nearest Underground
Piccadilly Circus 5 minutes
Green Park 7 minutes

www.paxtonandwhitfield.co.uk

Penhaligon's

13 The Piazza, Covent Garden,
WC2E 8RB

Founded in the late 1860s by William Henry Penhaligon, a Cornish barber who moved to London and became perfumer to Queen Victoria. The company received its first royal warrant in 1903 from Queen Alexandra and has remained a popular choice with the royal households. Penhaligon's held royal warrants for the Duke of Edinburgh, and King Charles when Prince of Wales with toilet requisites.

Princess Diana was fond of Penhaligon's Bluebell fragrance, while Winston Churchill used Blenheim Bouquet. All the perfumes are made and bottled in England and sold worldwide, with ranges including fragrances inspired by the British coastline.

Opening hours
Monday to Saturday 9am – 7pm
Sundays 10am – 5.30 pm

www.penhaligons.com

Prestat

14 Princes Arcade, Piccadilly, SW1Y 6DS

Chocolate truffles are a speciality of Prestat, a luxury chocolatier based in the Princes Arcade. Located on the south side of Piccadilly, almost opposite the Royal Academy of Arts, Princes Arcade links Piccadilly with Jermyn Street and houses a variety of boutique shops including menswear, health and wellness and a milliner.

In 1895, the Dufour family created the first chocolate truffles. Soon afterwards, Antoine Dufour moved from France to London and set up a business in Princes Arcade making and selling chocolate truffles. Over the years, these truffles became extremely popular, with many famous customers including Sir John Gielgud, Dame Peggy Ashcroft and Roald Dahl, creator of Willy Wonka.

Prestat's historic store in Princes Arcade.

The official letter from the Lord Chamberlain's office granting Prestat a royal warrant.

Royal photos on display among the chocolate.

Prestat was a supplier to Queen Elizabeth II between 1975-2022, and also supplied the Queen Mother. According to the owners, the Queen Mother encouraged them to be more adventurous in their packaging and admired the art deco style they devised.

The range on offer is extensive, including London gin and Black Forest truffles, liquorice fudge, chocolate mints, gourmet chocolates, rose and violet crèmes, chocolate dipped orange slices, and bars of chocolate. Special chocolates are made at Easter and Christmas.

According to a story in the *Daily Express*, the store's Easter offering did cause some concern at Buckingham

Palace. Apparently, Prestat sent Queen Elizabeth II a large handmade Easter Egg every year as a gift. Prestat's owner Nick Crean commented, 'You have to write to the Palace and say "your Majesty, we would like to present you with an egg", and they always reply saying, "We would very much like to receive an egg."'

One year, they forgot to send the egg.

'On the Monday morning before Easter, I got a call saying, "Hello, this is the Lady in Waiting to the Queen." When I realised it was real and said, "Oh, can I help you?" she said, "Yes I think you can. Where is our egg?" Oh my goodness, I knew exactly where it was, and I said we would get it to Buckingham Palace immediately. But the nice thing about it is that they really wanted the egg!'

Dark chocolate was a particular favourite of Queen Elizabeth II, especially dark chocolate wafers. Trial boxes were often sent to the Royal Family for feedback. Nick Crean says, 'We sent the first box to the Queen to try and got a letter back from the palace saying they had disappeared upstairs and never came back down again.'

Opening hours
Monday to Friday 9.30am – 6pm
Saturday 10am – 5pm
Sunday 11am – 4.30pm

Nearest Underground
Piccadilly Circus 4 minutes
Green Park 6 minutes

www.prestat.co.uk

Pringle Of Scotland

94 Mount Street, W1K 2SZ

Holders of a royal warrant from Queen Elizabeth II since 1956, Pringle of Scotland have a close relationship with the royal household. An exhibition celebrating their 200th anniversary held at the National Museum Edinburgh revealed some fascinating royal items from their archives. Every year, Queen Elizabeth II received an item of Pringle knitwear, and sent a thank you letter in response. She did this continually from 1947, when she received the first item as a twenty-one-year-old uncrowned princess. Another note from Clarence House was written by the Dresser to HM The Queen Mother simply requesting 'new cardigan please'. A photograph on display showed a sweater with a corgi on it made for Princess Anne.

Pringle are well known worldwide for cashmere products and knitwear. Traditionally they have focused on sweaters, cardigans and twinsets, but now include various high fashion items, hoodies, menswear and womenswear. The Argyll pattern was created by Pringle, and became instantly fashionable when the Duke of Windsor adopted the pattern in the 1920s.

Opening hours
Monday to Saturday 10am – 6.30pm

Nearest Underground
Bond Street 6 minutes

www.pringlescotland.com

Queen's Chapel Of The Savoy

Savoy Hill, WC2R ODA

Easily overlooked by visitors, this is tucked away at the side of the Savoy Hotel. It is all that remains of King Henry VII's sixteenth-century charitable foundation to provide accommodation for '100 poor and nedie men'. The original buildings included a massive hall and three chapels, built on the site of medieval royal prince John of Gaunt's Savoy Palace. Nothing of that palace now remains. King Henry's foundation was dissolved in 1702, and the majority of the buildings were demolished in the early nineteenth century to provide access for Waterloo Bridge.

In May 1937, King George VI (Queen Elizabeth's father) ordered that the Chapel of St John the Baptist on Savoy Hill should become the chapel of the Royal Victorian Order. Queen Victoria had founded the Royal Victorian Order in 1896, and it is awarded at the discretion of the sovereign. It is used to recognise various services given to the sovereign and the Royal Family. In 2019, Queen Elizabeth II appointed Kate Middleton as a Dame Grand Cross of the Royal Victorian Order, the highest rank possible. She wore the blue and gold sash with a Maltese cross on her hip for the first time at the state banquet held during the visit of the President of the USA. Other royal family members bearing the rank are Queen Consort Camilla and Sophie, Countess of Wessex. Prince Philip also held the rank. The Princess Royal is Grand Master of the Order.

The chapel hosts weddings and baptisms of members of the Order and their families.

Free entry

Opening hours
Monday to Thursday 9am – 4 pm
Closed Friday and Saturday
Sunday 9am – 1pm for worship only

Nearest Underground
Embankment 5 minutes
Covent Garden 5 minutes

www.royalchapelsavoy.org

Regent Street

W1B 4EA

One of the premier shopping streets of London, it was laid out in the early nineteenth century by architect John Nash. Named after George, the Prince Regent (later George IV), it occupies a long curve of Grade 2 listed shop façades located between Piccadilly Circus and Oxford Circus. This is the home of many iconic and prestigious brands such as Hamleys, Liberty, Burberry, Zara, Michael Kors, Aquascutum, Levi's and Watches of Switzerland. Mappin & Webb were jewellers, goldsmiths and silversmiths to Queen Elizabeth II, and also silversmiths to the King Charles when Prince of Wales. They have held royal warrants to five sovereigns including Queen Victoria.

The curving elegance of Regent Street on a busy day in London.

At Christmas time, Regent Street takes on an extra special appeal as it is always decorated in thousands of lights. The design changes each year and several members of the Royal Family have undertaken the ceremony of switching on the lights:

1987 – HRH Prince Edward
1986 – HRH Duchess Of York
1984 – HRH Prince Michael of Kent
1983 – HRH Princess Alexandra
1982 – HRH Prince Andrew
1981 – HRH Princess Diana
1979 – HRH Princess Michael of Kent
1978 – HRH Prince of Wales

Night time on Regent Street in the heart of London's West End.

Relaxing dining in Heddon Street, one of Regent Street's side streets.

Nearest Underground
Piccadilly Circus 2 minutes
Oxford Circus 3 minutes

www.regentstreetonline.com

Ritz Hotel

Piccadilly, W1J 9ER

Opulent and lavish, The Ritz is a byword for luxury worldwide. It has been one of the most prestigious hotels in the world ever since it first opened in 1906. The Ritz quickly gained an illustrious patron – the future King Edward VII – who is reputed to have said, 'Where Ritz goes, I go.' During the Second World War, Winston Churchill, Dwight Eisenhower and Charles de Gaulle used the Marie Antoinette suite to discuss military operations. More recently, it was used for filming scenes for the acclaimed TV drama, Downton Abbey.

In 2002, Charles, then Prince of Wales granted the Ritz a royal warrant for its banqueting and catering Services. That same year, Queen Elizabeth II hosted a party in the Ritz Restaurant for the Prince of Wales' fifty-fourth birthday. In 2006, Queen Elizabeth II celebrated her eightieth birthday at the Ritz.

Whatever the reason for visiting the Ritz, it is guaranteed to be an experience. Check the dress code before visiting –jeans and trainers are not acceptable for afternoon tea, while men must wear a jacket and tie. Immaculately uniformed doormen guide you into the hotel, and you walk over deep, luxurious carpets to reach the mirrored Palm Court with its pink and gold décor for a superb afternoon tea. Glittering chandeliers hang overhead, as musicians play nearby. Drink tea that is sourced directly from the best plantations, enjoy delicate cakes and sandwiches served on a three-tiered tray by attentive staff. Dining in the Michelin starred Ritz Restaurant is a feast of British seasonal ingredients. On Friday and Saturday evening, diners can enjoy fine dining with live entertainment and the opportunity to dance the night away.

Nearest Underground
Green Park 2 minutes
Piccadilly Circus 8 minutes

www.theritzlondon.com

Royal Academy Of Art

Burlington House, Piccadilly, W1J 0BD

Royal links go back to the very foundation of the Royal Academy of Art. It was in 1768 that King George II signed the foundation document to create an institution that would focus on the visual arts and architecture through the medium of education, exhibitions and debates. He became the Royal Academy's first patron, and this royal patronage has continued over the years. Queen Elizabeth was 'patron, protector and supporter' of the Royal Academy, a role now taken by King Charles III. During Queen Elizabeth's visit in 2018, she viewed an exhibition on Charles I as King and Collector, before walking to the new building and unveiling the first painting to be installed *in situ* – a self portrait by the Royal Academy's first president,

The Royal Academy of Art has been associated with the monarchy since 1768.

Sir Joshua Reynolds. Other royal visits by Queen Elizabeth included her diamond jubilee celebrations in 2012, and a reception as part of her ninetieth birthday celebrations.

The Royal Academy possesses an extensive collection of art works created by previous and existing Royal Academicians. Among the collection are works by Constable, Dame Laura Knight, Tracy Emin and Millais. Every summer there is an open exhibition featuring works by professional and amateur artists as well as Royal Academicians. Other exhibitions range from Old Masters such as Gauguin and the Impressionists to modern artists like Antony Gormley and Finnish artist Helene Schjerfbeck.

Free entry to the main collection, but some exhibitions may be charged.

Opening hours
10am – 6pm daily
Friday late opening until 10pm

Nearest Underground
Piccadilly Circus 6 minutes
Green Park 5 minutes

www.royalacademy.org.uk

Savile Row

Mayfair, W1S 3PG

Saville Row is a long street running parallel to Regent Street, linked into Sackville Street, and known as the centre of bespoke tailoring in London.

Built in the Palladian style during the mid eighteenth century, Savile Row's reputation grew quickly. Sometimes described as the 'golden mile of tailoring', Savile Row has attracted numerous high profile customers including Lord Nelson, Winston Churchill and Jude Law. Nutters attracted Mick Jagger, the Beatles, Elton John and Andrew Lloyd Webber.

Among its early tailors was Henry Poole, inventor of the dinner jacket, based on a smoking jacket he designed for the Prince of Wales (later Edward VII) in 1860.

Royal warrant holders are much in evidence and include Henry Poole, Gieves & Hawkes, Dege & Skinner, and Bernard Weatherill, while Meyer & Mortimer provided the Queen's military uniforms. Anderson & Sheppard and Gieves & Hawkes held warrants from Prince Charles when Prince of Wales, while Gieves & Hawkes and John Pegg served the Duke of Edinburgh.

In the late 1960s Savile Row was the headquarters of The Beatles Apple Corp. They recorded *Let it Be* in a studio built in the basement of 3 Savile Row. In 1969, they gave their last public performance with a concert held on the rooftop of the building, recording it for the *Let It Be* documentary – at least until the performance was stopped by the police.

Nearest Underground
Oxford Circus 6 minutes

Savoy Hotel

The Strand, WC2R OEZ

Perfectly positioned within walking distance of London's West End and Covent Garden, as well as luxury shopping in Mayfair, the Savoy Hotel is the only luxury hotel overlooking the river Thames. Now over 130 years old, the Savoy is renowned for its memorable experiences such as delicious afternoon tea accompanied by live music, in a wood-panelled dining room under a large glass dome. At night the foyer transforms into a setting reminiscent of the 1920s jazz age, with diners sitting back and enjoying live entertainment from singers and musicians.

Built by Victorian impresario Richard D'Oyly Carte using the profits from his Gilbert and Sullivan opera productions, especially *The Mikado*. It was the first luxury hotel in Britain and immediately attracted a lot of attention due to the fact that it was the first such building to have electric lighting everywhere, *en suite* bathrooms, constant hot and cold running water, as well as electric lifts.

Edward VII was one of the first visitors to the hotel, and became a frequent guest. It has continued to be a popular destination for members of the royal family. Princess Elizabeth and Princess Margaret often came to enjoy dinner and dancing in the 1940s. It is where the romance blossoming between Princess Elizabeth and Prince Philip of Greece first came to public attention. During a wedding reception, Princess Elizabeth the chief bridesmaid was photographed in the company of a young man in uniform – Prince Philip. They were at this point already engaged, but no one outside the family knew. Since then, they have celebrated several wedding anniversaries at the Savoy within a private dining room.

The lavish interior of the Savoy Hotel.

Taking afternoon tea at the Savoy.

Wearing an eye-catching sparkling pale blue dress with a slight bustle, Princess Diana attended the 1989 Savoy Centenary Ball in aid of Birthright, a charity of which she was patron. Prince Charles, then Prince of Wales undertook the official reopening of the Savoy Hotel, following its restoration in 2010. Seven years later, a large portrait of Queen Elizabeth II by Henry Ward was unveiled in the Upper Thames Foyer. The portrait had been commissioned by the Red Cross to mark her role as patron of the charity for the past six decades.

Virtually every member of the royal family has been to the Savoy, whether for a public or a private event. Viscount Linley (son of Princess Margaret) created the furniture for the restoration of the front hall in 1996, while the Queen Mother even opened the renovated and refitted restaurant kitchen during the 1980s, reflecting the frequency with which she used to pop in for lunch.

Nearest Underground

Charing Cross 4 minutes
Embankment 6 minutes

www.thesavoylondon.com

Selfridges

400 Oxford Street, W1A 1AB

Located at the Marble Arch end of Oxford Street, Selfridges is one of the biggest and oldest department stores in London, second only to Harrods in size. Founded by an American entrepreneur named Harry Gordon Selfridge, the store has always aimed to make shopping a fun adventure, and a leisure activity rather than a chore. It was the first store to put merchandise on display for customers to examine, as well as holding free exhibitions of educational and scientific items such as Louis Bleriot's monoplane as a way of encouraging people to enter the store. It has been voted the best department store in the world several times and held a royal warrant from Queen Elizabeth II as a supplier of food and household goods.

There are over 300 departments, including fashion, home, beauty, toys, food, luxury brands, food, restaurants, cafés and 'one of a kind luxury experiences'. There is also a cinema within the Oxford Street store.

Princess Beatrice worked as a personal shopper in Selfridges for a month during her gap year and it has remained one of her favourite stores. She recommends the Mad Hatter's Afternoon Tea experience on her Pinterest site.

Opening hours
Monday to Saturday 10am – 7pm
Sundays 11am – 5pm

Nearest Underground
Bond Street 2 minutes
Marble Arch 7 minutes

www.selfridges.com

Smythson Of Bond Street

131 – 132 New Bond Street, W1S 2TB

For over 130 years Smythson have been creating superb luxury leather goods. Frank Smythson opened his first store in 1887 and he soon began to supply stationery to Queen Victoria. Smythson received its first royal warrant in 1964 from Queen Elizabeth II and subsequently gained a royal warrant from the Duke of Edinburgh. The company creates a wide range of leather goods including notebooks and fashion accessories. The Princess of Wales is a keen user of Smythson products. She was seen using a Smythson folder to contain her speech notes when attending the Back to Nature Festival at Wisley. During the royal tour of Pakistan she used a Smythson Tote Bag, and on other occasions has been seen with a Smythson Panama clutch bag and a Ludlow Concertina Crossbody bag. The Duchess of Sussex sent Smythson personalised leather notebooks as thank you gifts to her *Vogue* contributors in 2019.

Opening hours
Monday to Wednesday and Friday
    9.30am – 6pm
Thursday 10am – 7pm
Saturday 10am – 6pm

Nearest Underground
Bond Street 5 minutes

www.smythson.com

Spink & Son

69 Southampton Row, Bloomsbury, WC1B 4ET

Philatelist to Queen Elizabeth II, Spink & Son is a leading auction house specialising in the sale of stamps, coins, banknotes, medals, autographs, books and fine wines. Auctions are held regularly.

Nearest Underground
Russell Square 6 minutes
Holborn 5 minutes

www.spink.com

Stanley Gibbons

399 Strand, WC2R 0LX

Royal warrant holders Stanley Gibbons were stamp merchants to Queen Elizabeth II. Their store on the Strand is a collector's paradise. On sale are catalogues, books, accessories and over 3,000,000 stamps, including many rare and valuable ones.

Around ten auctions are held every year. It is the only company specialising purely in everything to do with stamps, and has been publishing stamp magazines since 1890.

King George V granted the first royal warrant in 1914. It held a royal warrant from Queen Elizabeth between 1956-2022. In 1977, Stanley Gibbons was awarded a Queens Award to Industry for outstanding export achievements.

Opening hours
Monday to Friday 9am – 5.30pm
Saturday 9.30am – 5.30pm

Nearest Underground
Covent Garden 5 minutes
Embankment 7 minutes

www.stanleygibbons.com

Stamp merchants to the Queen, this is the Stanley Gibbons store on the Strand.

The stamp auction room at Stanley Gibbons.

Buying stamps at Stanley Gibbons, with its royal warrant prominently displayed.

St Mary Le Strand

Strand, WC2R 1ES

This eighteenth century church is a prominent London landmark possessing a commanding view down the Strand. It has been described as one of the loveliest London Baroque churches. St Mary's has a stunning, highly decorative plaster ceiling and was designed to make the most of Queen Anne's regular use of the route from St James's Palace to St Pauls. Motifs on the facades were inspired by the royal processions.

In 1984, it became the church of the WRNS, Women's Royal Naval Service, often known as the Wrens. The WRNS was formed in 1917 to 'free a man for sea' and became part of the Royal Navy in 1993. The church is supported by the Association of Wrens and Women of the Royal Naval Services. The Princess Royal is patron of the Association of Wrens and attended the 1993 WRNS Carol Service. New displays seek to bring the work of the Wrens to life.

Opening hours
Tuesday to Thursday 12 noon-4pm

Nearest Underground
Temple 5 minutes
Covent Garden

St Clement Danes RAF Church

Strand, WC2R 1DH

It is hard to miss St Clement Danes church as you walk along the Strand towards Fleet Street. Just outside the Royal Courts of Justice, the Strand suddenly divides into two around this island church. Not only that, when you listen to the bells they play the children's nursery rhyme, *Oranges and Lemons*.

There has been a church on this spot for over 1,200 years. Sir Christopher Wren built the existing church 330 years ago. Bombs destroyed much of the church during the London Blitz in the Second World War. After restoration had been completed in 1958, it was consecrated as the Central Church of the RAF in the presence of Queen Elizabeth II and Duke of Edinburgh.

The church is a perpetual shrine of remembrance for those killed on active service in the RAF, as well as Allied Air Forces during the Second World War. Virtually every inch of the church is covered in memorials to airmen, with commonwealth crests and RAF unit badges inlaid on the floor of the nave. In the centre of the floor is the Battle of Britain Flight crest. Banners and colour standards adorn the walls. In 1992, the Queen Mother unveiled a statue of Hugh Dowding, chief of RAF Fighter Command in the Battle of Britain just outside the church.

The Princess of Wales is the Royal Patron of the RAF Air Cadets and visited the church in 2016 for a service marking the seventy-fifth anniversary of the RAF Air Cadets. Her clothes matched the theme perfectly as she wore an Alexander McQueen cornflower blue coat dress.

Opening hours

10am – 4pm daily

Closed Bank Holiday Mondays and
between 26 December and the first
working day of the New Year

Nearest Underground

Temple 3 minutes
Chancery Lane 7 minutes

Mainline Train

City Thameslink 9 minutes
Blackfriars 9 minutes

www.stclementdanesraf.org

Theatre Royal Drury Lane

Catherine Street, Covent Garden, WC2B 5JF

Usually known quite simply as Drury
Lane, royal connections go back to
the seventeenth century and the very
first theatre to built on this spot. Nell
Gwynne used to tread the boards here,
watched by her lover King Charles II.
Drury Lane is the oldest theatre in
London still in daily use. The current
Grade 1 listed building is the fourth to
be built here. Drury Lane is a well-
known location for musicals, especially
ones with long runs. In 1989, Diana,
Princess of Wales wore a sparkling pale
blue chiffon Catherine Walker evening
gown with long matching scarf to watch
a performance of *Miss Saigon*. In 2017,
it was the turn of the Princess of Wales,
when attending the opening night of
Broadway musical *42nd Street* in her
role as patron of EACH, the East Anglian
Children's Hospice.

Drury Lane has hosted the Royal
Variety Performance on four occasions,
between 1979 and 1991. On each
occasion, the royal guest was Queen
Elizabeth II.

Watch carefully when visiting Drury
Lane, as you may encounter more than
anticipated. This is said to be one of
the world's most haunted theatres,
which is not surprising given its links
with regicide plots, fires and wartime
bombings. Between 2019 – 2020, the
theatre underwent a major restoration
project designed to restore it to its 1812
glory, while providing better sightlines
and new seating.

Theatre tours are held regularly
enabling people to explore backstage
and discover hidden tales of tragedy,
bankruptcy and murder. No two tours
are ever the same, as routes backstage
vary according to what is happening at
the time.

Tours and performances should be pre-
booked.

Nearest Underground

Covent Garden 5 minutes
Holborn 8 minutes

www.lwtheatres.co.uk

Turnbull & Asser

71/72 Jermyn Street, St James, SW1

In 1982, Turnbull & Asser received the
first royal warrant issued by Prince
Charles, Prince of Wales soon after
his official investiture. The company

is responsible for fitting King Charles III whenever he needs a new shirt. In 2013 he visited the Gloucester factory responsible for manufacturing all Turnbull & Asser shirts.

Each bespoke shirt is made from thirty-four pieces of cloth, with at least ten mother-of-pearl buttons. Ties are also handmade using exclusive silks and indestructible thread. Apart from the bespoke service, the company also produce a range of ready to wear shirts and ties. Turnbull & Asser have been making shirts since 1885 using only traditional skills and craftspeople. One of their most popular ranges uses a check popularised by Prince Charles, known as the blue Prince of Wales check.

Other famous clients include Pablo Picasso, Charlie Chaplin and Twiggy. The company's products have appeared on film as Turnbull & Asser created Sean Connery's *Dr No* Shirt for the debut James Bond film and all later James Bond films, and Colin Firth's shirts in *Kingsman*. Having provided the shirts for Daniel Craig's role as James Bond in *Casino Royale*, they had to visit his hotel during the worldwide premiere tour in order to measure for a bespoke sling to match his dress suit as he had broken his arm. During the Second World War, Churchill commissioned Turnbull & Asser to make his famous siren suit.

Jermyn Street is a historic location, home to tailors, art galleries and restaurants. It has always had strong royal links, as the street dates back to 1664 when Charles II gave Lord Henry Jermyn, Earl of St Albans, the right to develop the area close to St James's Palace.

Opening hours
9am – 6pm daily
Thursday 9am – 7pm
Sunday closed

Nearest Underground
Piccadilly Circus 4 minutes
Green Park 7 minutes

www.turnbullandasser.co.uk

R. Twining & Company
216 The Strand, WC2R 1AP

The world's first dry tea and coffee shop was opened by Thomas Twining in 1706 – and is still open today. This is now the oldest teashop in London, being over 300 years old. It is also the oldest shop in Westminster trading on the same site, owned by the same family and selling the same product continuously, making it a unique store.

Located directly opposite the Royal Courts of Justice, it is a tea lover's dream. Catherine of Braganza introduced tea into England when she married King Charles II. It quickly became a fashionable drink and has maintained its popularity. Jane Austen wrote in her diary that her mother sent her to London to pick up a supply of Twinings tea.

The oldest teashop in London, dating back over 300 years.

Twinings has always led the way in tea. In 1831, it invented Earl Grey tea and was awarded its first royal warrant by Queen Victoria in 1837. Twinings has supplied every British monarch since then and is officially tea and Coffee merchants to both Queen Elizabeth II and King Charles III. In 2016, Twinings created a special Queen Elizabeth ninetieth birthday tea.

A wide range of teas and other products can be purchased in store, and you can also try samples of various teas. There is a loose tea bar and you can sign up for masterclasses in tea.

Try out the teas at Twinings original store.

Relax with a cup of tea in the teashop after exploring the museum of tea and Twinings.

Nearest Underground
Temple 5 minutes
Chancery Lane 5 minutes

www.twinings.co.uk

Wallace Collection

Hertford House, Manchester Square, W1U 3BN

Sophie, Countess of Wessex is patron of the Wallace Collection and has attended various events including hosting a gala at Buckingham Palace celebration the bicentenary year of Lady Wallace's birth.

Created by Sir Richard Wallace during the eighteenth and nineteenth centuries, the collection is outstanding. It contains a wide range of objects relating to fine and decorative arts from the fifteenth to nineteenth centuries especially paintings, furniture, arms, armour, porcelain, Limoges enamels, maijolica and glassware. Among the notable Old Master paintings on display are works by Titian, Van Dyke, Rembrandt, Frans Hals, Gainsborough and Delacroix.

Opening hours
10am – 5 pm daily

Nearest Underground
Baker Street 4 minutes
Bond Street 7 minutes

www.wallacecollection.org

NORTH LONDON

Abbey Road Studios

Abbey Road, NW8 9AY

A rainy February day in 2020 saw Prince Harry undertaking one of his final engagements as a working royal, joining Jon Bon Jovi and the Invictus Games Choir to record a charity record at the Abbey Road Studios, in aid of the Invictus Games Foundation.

Prince Harry is one of many celebrities and musicians who have entered these studios. By far the best known of all are the Beatles, who were photographed walking across the zebra crossing outside, in a scene which has become one of the most iconic in the world. Almost all of the Beatles songs were recorded here.

Abbey Road Studios has always been a landmark in music history. This was the location of the first purpose-built recording studio in the world when work began on site in 1928. Sir Edward Elgar conducted a performance of Land of Hope and Glory as part of the opening ceremony three years later. Since then countless musicians and singers have recorded at this site, including Cliff Richard, Shirley Bassey, Pink Floyd and Aretha Franklin.

There are no studio tours available, but you can leave messages on the graffiti wall at the front of the studios and visit the Abbey Road shop. Alternatively of course, recreate the famous walk across the zebra crossing just like Prince Harry and Jon Bon Jovi!

Nearest Underground
St John's Wood 5 minutes walk

www.abbeyroad.com

Alexandra Palace

Alexandra Palace Way, N22 7AY

'Alexandra Palace is one of the coolest places in London. Once the lighting building for London in Victorian times, this landmark hosts conferences and events' states Princess Eugenie on her Instagram site. It has become one of her favourite places.

A popular venue for musical performances spanning all styles of music, it also offers talks, dances, restaurants, cafés, comedy and events such as antiques and collectors fairs. There is a large ice rink, garden centre, play area, boating lake and a Go Ape treetops adventure centre along with beautiful grounds perfect for walking and playing.

The Alexandra Palace was built in 1863, and almost immediately destroyed by fire. The Palace was rebuilt and eventually reopened in 1875. Nicknamed the Ally Pally, it has always been a favourite place of Londoners wanting somewhere to relax and be entertained. In those early years, Londoners could enjoy all kinds of activities, including a theatre, racetrack, circus and boating lake, strolling in the extensive parkland plus dining on site. Other buildings within the Alexandra Palace grounds have included the site of the world's first television service in 1936, leading to the studios becoming the home of TV news. It was the original home of the Open University. A major programme of restoration is underway, designed to bring all the derelict spaces at Alexandra Palace back to life.

Opening hours

East Court: 9am – 5pm daily dependent on events

Parkland: 24 hours a day

Nearest Train

Alexandra Palace 14 minutes

Nearest Underground

Wood Green 23 minutes (via Park)

www.alexandrapalace.com

Arsenal

Drayton Park, N5 1BU

One of London's premier football clubs, Arsenal was originally based at Highbury, north London. It moved to a new purpose-built stadium capable of seating 60,704 people in 2006. Originally the new stadium was due to be opened by Queen Elizabeth II but she was unable to do so due to a back injury. Prince Philip took her place and performed the opening ceremony. Prince Harry is said to have watched a number of games here, as he is an Arsenal fan. Apparently Queen Elizabeth II was also an Arsenal supporter!

Apart from watching games, visitors are welcome at the Stadium. Guarding the entrance is a statue of Herbert Chapman, regarded as one of the greatest visionaries of the English game. He was responsible for numerous innovations, including the renaming of the nearest tube station, 'Gillespie Road' to 'Arsenal' so that the club's name appears on the tube map. He also suggested the concept of a floodlit pitch, shirt numbers and the penalty area arc design.

Different types of guided tours are available – self guided stadium tours and guided Matchday, Legend and VIP Legend Experience tours. These are a fun way to see behind the scenes as you can go pitchside, visit the Directors' Box, see the interview rooms and walk through the players' tunnel. On Match Days, you may even be lucky enough to see players preparing for a match, or taking fitness tests. All tours must be pre-booked.

The statue of football legend Herbert Chapman outside Arsenal's Emirates Stadium.

Explore the history of Arsenal with a guided stadium tour.

Opening hours
10am – 5pm weekdays
Saturday 9:30am – 6pm
Sunday 10am – 4pm

Nearest Underground
Arsenal 5 minutes

Nearest Train
Finsbury Park/Highbury and Islington
   10 minutes

www.arsenal.com

British Library

Euston Road, St Pancras, NW1 2DB

'An academy for secret police' is how King Charles III described plans for the British Library – despite this, he still laid the foundation stone! The new purpose-built building was essential, as the Library had outgrown its original home at the British Museum.

The British Library was founded in 1753. Charles Dickens, Charles Darwin, Karl Marx and Lenin were among the many famous people who used its iconic round Reading Room. The new British Library building was opened by Queen Elizabeth II in June 1997, and was the largest public building to be created in over a century. It contains one of the largest collections of books, manuscripts, periodicals both British and foreign, in the world, including many rare books. Over 1.6m visitors come here every year either to use the various reading rooms or to attend one of the many exhibitions, talks, lectures and masterclasses. Some of these events are free to attend, while others require payment. The subject matter is extensive, ranging from Harry Potter, Elizabeth I and Mary Queen of

The British Library contains a massive collection of books, manuscripts and periodicals.

Scots, Japanese textile designs, and Hebrew manuscripts. The Treasures of the British Library exhibition covered everything from the Magna Carta to the Beatles.

Opening hours
Monday to Thursday 9.30am – 8pm
Friday 9.30am – 6pm
Saturday 9.30am – 5pm
Sunday 11am – 5pm

Nearest Underground
St Pancras/Kings Cross 5 minutes
Euston 5 minutes

www.bl.uk

Lords Cricket Ground

St John's Wood Road, St John's Wood, NW8 8QN

For cricket fans, Marylebone Cricket Club's Lords Cricket Ground is the doyen of cricket venues, home of the iconic Ashes Urn, and where countless cricketing legends have played over the past hundred years. In 2013, Queen Elizabeth II walked out onto the legendary pitch to meet the England and Australian teams taking part in the second Ashes Test Match. Three years later, Prince Harry showed off his cricketing skills when he attended an event marking the expansion of the Coach Core sports coaching apprenticeship scheme designed by the Royal Foundation. In 2017, the Duke of Edinburgh, a honorary life member of the Marylebone Cricket Club, opened the Warner Stand at the Club.

Non-members can book a guided behind the scenes tour of Lords Cricket Ground. This provides the opportunity to see the famous Long Room, admire the elegant Pavilion and discover the

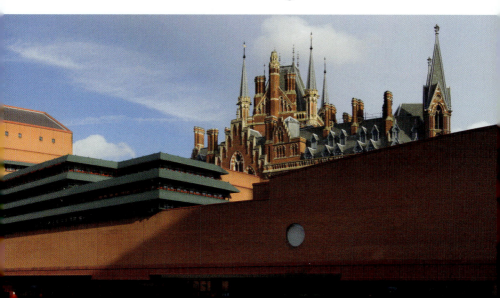

secrets of the dressing rooms as well as taking a look at the Ashes Urn in the MCC museum. Lots of other cricketing memorabilia is on display, such as Mrs Grace's teapot and Eoin Morgan's bat as well as numerous cricket related paintings.

For something slightly different, you can book a Players' Dining Room Experience allowing you to enjoy a three course meal within the Players' Dining Room. The menu is limited in choice – it is exactly the same one used by players on match days.

Alternatively, you can take the players' walk from the dressing room to the Lords turf with the aid of a cricketing icon, someone who has actually played on that turf and knows exactly what it is like to face the crowds on a match day.

Tours must be pre-booked and are held daily except on match days or event days. Times vary according to season but are generally between 10am – 3pm.

Nearest Underground
St John's Wood 5 minutes

www.lords.org

London Zoo

Outer circle, NW1 4RY

Tucked away in a corner of Regent's Park (another royal park), is London Zoo. It is sometimes called Regent's Zoo because of its location. The Zoo is actually the oldest in the world, and celebrates its 200th anniversary in 2026. It has several royal connections. In 1938, Queen Elizabeth II (then Princess Elizabeth) visited the zoo with her sister, Princess Margaret, to see the animals. In 1999, Queen Elizabeth and Prince Philip opened the Millennium Conservation centre with its BUGS biodiversity area. Eight years later, they came back to open the Gorilla Kingdom. In 2013 Prince Philip opened the Tiger Territory while in 2016 Queen Elizabeth II opened the Land of the Lions enclosure. King Charles III and the Prince of Wales have visited for discussions with conservation leaders.

It is an amazing place and enjoyment is guaranteed. There is a vast array of animals to be seen at the zoo including monkeys, lemurs, meerkats, mongoose,

London Zoo's legendary reptile house.

One of the lions living in the Land of the Lions enclosure opened by Queen Elizabeth II.

aardvarks, prairie dogs, kune kune pigs, llamas, alpacas, porcupines, donkeys, a Penguin beach, African bird safari and a reptile house which played a starring role in *Harry Potter and the Philosopher's Stone*. One of the okapi is named Meghan, having been born just after Prince Harry's engagement announcement.

Opening hours
10am daily except Christmas day
Closing times vary seasonally

Nearest Underground
Camden Town 15 minutes
Regent's Park 20 minutes

www.zsl.org

Luminary Bakery

71 – 73 Allen Road, Stoke Newington, Hackney, N16 8RY

47 Chalk Farm Road, Chalk Farm, Camden, NW1 8AJ

Casually dressed in jeans, the Duchess of Sussex carried out a low key visit to Luminary Bakery's new site in Camden to celebrate its opening, and donned an apron to help with cake decorating. Earlier in the year, she had featured the company as a force for change in her guest-edited *British Vogue* issue in 2019. Writing on Instagram, the Duchess commented 'While the baked goods are absolutely delicious, it's the story of how the programme at Luminary reshapes lives through baking that is the actual icing on the cake.'

Luminary is an all-women bakery company. It is a social enterprise business designed to encourage women to develop entrepreneurial and career skills by providing employment and training within a supportive community. The aim is to provide transferable job and business skills that will benefit women in their future careers.

Freshly baked food created on the premises is available all day, including breakfast and lunch options, cakes, snacks and bread. Special cake options can be ordered online. The bakery includes one of the Duchess' favourite meals – avocado on toast.

Opening hours
Hackney
Weekdays 8am – 5pm
Weekends 9am – 3.30pm

Camden
Weekends 8am – 5.30pm

Nearest Underground
Hackney
Stoke Newington 8 minutes
Arsenal 27 minutes

Camden
Chalk Farm 5 minutes
Camden town 8 minutes

www.luminarybakery.com

Madame Tussauds

Marylebone Road, NW1 5LR

This is the perfect royal photo opportunity – have an audience with King Charles III or stand beside Queen Elizabeth II on the balcony. Senior members of the Royal Family are always on view at Madame Tussauds, and are constantly being updated to reflect their age. The first version of Queen Elizabeth II was created when she was just two years old; the current model is the twenty-third to be made. King Charles III, Queen Consort Camilla, plus the Prince and Princess of Wales stand regally against an ornate palace style setting, while models of Queen Elizabeth II and Prince Philip stand on a replica of the Buckingham Palace balcony.

Interestingly, all the models have been created with the involvement of Buckingham Palace. When the last model of Queen Elizabeth II was being developed, the images of the clay head were sent to the palace for approval. Models of Prince Harry and Meghan Markle were rapidly removed from the display in early 2020 following their decision to stand down from royal duties.

Apart from royalty, this is also a great place to discover images of famous and historical people, TV and film stars, sports heroes and heroines. Serial killers lurk in the Chamber Gallery, where you can stand up to Sherlock

Meet the Royal Family and enjoy a photo opportunity at Madam Tussauds.

Queen Elizabeth II.

Holmes, and try out some dance moves in the music zone. Madame Tussauds has been the home of waxwork models for over a century and its models are incredibly realistic.

Opening hours
Monday 9am – 4pm
Tuesday to Saturday 9am – 5pm
Sunday 9am – 6pm

Nearest Underground
Baker Street 2 minutes

Nearest Train
Marylebone10 minutes

www.madametussauds.com

Paddington Station

Praed Street, Paddington, W2 1RH

While pregnant with Prince Louis, the Princess of Wales showed off her dance moves with Paddington Bear at the Station in a memorable event in 2017. Along with Prince William and Prince Harry, she was celebrating the launch of the *Paddington Bear* movie with kids involved in royal charities. This is, after all, Paddington's own station. It was here that Mr and Mrs Brown found Paddington when he arrived from darkest Peru, and took him to live with them, resulting in a lively series of children's books written by Michael Bond. A life-size bronze statue of Paddington can be found under the clock on Platform One – just where the Brown family found him. Michael Bond unveiled the statue in 2000. Follow the Pawprint trail around the area, or join a Paddington Bear walking tour. You can also do some shopping in the only specialist Paddington Bear shop, containing many exclusive items.

Paddington Station is one of the oldest mainline and underground stations in the world. It was original terminus of the first underground railway opened in 1863. Paddington was the grand terminus of Isambard Kingdom Brunel's Great Western Railway, providing train services to Bristol and beyond. Princess Anne, the Princess Royal is a regular passenger, *en route* to her home at Gatcombe Park,

Gloucestershire. In March 2020, she visited the station in an official capacity, as Commandant-in-Chief of the First Aid Nursery Yeomanry – a volunteer corps for women, which supplied many SOE operatives during the Second World War. The Princess Royal was naming a train Odette Hallowes, in memory of her work during the war as an SOE operative and member of FANY.

Nearest Underground
Paddington Station 1 minute

www.networkrail.co.uk/communities/passengers/our-stations/london-paddington

RAF Hendon

Grahame Park Way, NW9 5LL

Queen Elizabeth II opened the museum at RAF Hendon in 1972 and Prince Philip was its patron. 50 years later in 2022, she granted it a Royal Charter as part

The RAF Rescue helicopter flown by Prince William, Prince of Wales while on active service in Anglesey.

of its birthday celebrations. Prince William completed his RAF service flying helicopters out into the Atlantic on search and rescue missions. Based at RAF Valley, Anglesey, he took part in many missions. Soon after he left active service, his Westland helicopter also retired to RAF Hendon in north London. And it's not just his royal aircraft that can be seen here.

Also on display are the training aircraft used by King Charles III when he was learning to fly at RAF Cranwell and a Royal Wessex helicopter frequently used by Queen Elizabeth II on her travels. One of the first flights she made in the helicopter was in 1969 for the Prince of Wales' investiture in Caernarfon Castle, Wales.

The Royal Family's links with military flying stretch back to the dawn of aviation when King Edward VII met the Wright brothers in Paris. By 1916, the Prince of Wales became the first royal prince to make a flight in an aircraft. Two years later, he went up in a plane with Major Barker who flew with one arm in a sling! Horrified, the King prohibited the Prince of Wales from flying – his brother, Prince Albert (later George VI and Queen Elizabeth's father), promptly transferred to the RAF and took flying lessons. A King's Flight was established at RAF Hendon, and in 1953 Prince Philip took the first royal flight in a helicopter.

Exploring RAF Hendon is definitely a voyage of discovery into flight as well as RAF history. There are numerous unique planes ranging from flimsy Royal Aircraft Factory BE2b reconnaissance planes to a rare Sunderland flying boat, from a prototype Typhoon to a Messerschmitt. Find out how planes were designed and built, try making a virtual plane and seeing if it will fly, join the Dambusters on their legendary mission, soar through the air with the Red Arrows and sit in the controls of a Spitfire. Try on RAF uniforms, and discover how many crafts are needed to make one modern plane fly. Special events are held throughout the summer.

Entry is free, but some activities are charged.

Opening hours
10am – 5pm daily

Nearest Underground
Colindale 10 minutes

www.rafmuseum.org.uk

The Westland Helicopter used by Queen Elizabeth when attending the Prince Charles investiture as Prince of Wales at Caernarfon Castle in 1969.

St Pancras International

Euston Road, Kings Cross, N1C 4QP

This is probably one of the best known of all London railway stations due to Harry and Ron's flying car scene in *Harry Potter and the Chamber of Secrets*. St Pancras is a masterpiece of Victorian engineering, from its layout to Sir George Gilbert Scott's dramatic Victorian gothic façade, which is now a five-star hotel. Nearly 60 million bricks were used to construct St Pancras and its approach routes, resulting in the creation of the largest enclosed space in the world. Nowadays, it has more shops than any other railway station, together with a fresh produce market, gastro pubs and the longest champagne bar at 93 metres (300 feet). Free live music and poetry events provide passenger entertainment. Several pianos scattered around the station encourage anyone to have a go – resulting in impromptu performances by passing celebrities like Elton John and Jools Holland.

St Pancras is now the terminus for Eurostar, with regular services to Paris, Brussels and Amsterdam. The station underwent an £800m transformation which included the creation of the new Eurostar rail terminal, resulting in the revamped facilities being opened by Queen Elizabeth II and Duke of Edinburgh in 2007.

The Princess of Wales has been seen using St Pancras on several occasions, most notably in 2012 when she accompanied Queen Elizabeth and Duke of Edinburgh to Leicester as part of the Diamond Jubilee royal tour.

Nearest Underground
Kings Cross St Pancras 1 minute

www.stpancras.com

Warner Bros. Studio Tour – The Making of Harry Potter

Leavesden, Watford, WD25 7LR

Who could resist the chance of flourishing wands for a wizarding duel? The Prince & Princess of Wales certainly

One of the wizarding stores in Diagon Alley, part of the Warner Bros. Studio Tour opened by the Prince & Princess of Wales.

couldn't during their visit to the Harry Potter studio tour in 2013. Along with Prince Harry and around 500 children, they had great fun launching the studio complex. The giant figure of Hagrid positively towered over Kate, while all three royals were delighted when they received their own wands and began some spell practice standing outside Scribbulus in Diagon Alley. Elsewhere, Prince Harry was seen on the set of the Weasley family home.

Since that initial launch, thousands of visitors have poured through the doors of the Warner Brothers Studio tour, all keen to follow in the royal footsteps. Step on board the Hogwarts Express, meet the dreaded spider Aragog, discover the secrets of green screen filming and fly a broomstick or walk through the Forbidden Forest. Brave the darkness of Professor Snape's Potions Room, admire the splendour of the Great Hall, see Dumbledore's Study and marvel at Gringotts giant security door while imagining yourself as a member of the Gryffindor Common Room. Special exhibitions are sometimes held, for example Hogwarts in the Snow at Christmas or decorated for Halloween.

Timed slot entry tickets must be pre-booked, but once through the Great Hall you can spend as much time as you want within the displays.

Opening hours
Vary depending on the season

Nearest Train
Watford Junction, shuttle bus to site takes 15 minutes
Direct bus transfers from Kings Cross and Victoria

www.wbstudiotour.co.uk

Wembley Stadium

Wembley, HA9 0WS

Football fan Prince William has often visited Wembley to watch matches, as well as to undertake his annual task as Patron of the Football Association of presenting the FA Cup at the Championship match. It was here that

The eye catching Weasleys' Wizard Wheezes joke shop in Diagon Alley.

he was pictured in 2020 holding his head in his hands after watching his beloved Aston Villa team lose in the Carabao Cup Final. This was the venue for the Concert for Diana in 2007 attended by Princes William and Harry, while in 2019 Prince Harry and Meghan Markle attended the Young Leaders WE Day.

The royal links started as long ago as 1924, when King George V (Queen Elizabeth II's grandfather) opened the stadium.

Wembley Stadium hosts numerous major sporting events, as well as music concerts. Typical events have included the 1948 Olympic Games, the 1966 FIFA World Cup and the Rugby League Challenge Cup. It is a massive stadium, seating 90,000 people for sporting events.

Apart from attending events here, you can book special guided tours such as the Behind the Scenes Tour and the VIP Matchday tours. These offer opportunities to sit in the royal box, go pitchside through the players tunnel, lift a replica FA cup and walk in the footsteps of football legends. You can even climb the 107 Trophy Winners steps to reach the royal box!

The onsite café and shop is open daily.

Nearest Underground
Wembley Stadium 5 minutes

www.wembleystadium.com

6

CITY OF LONDON

Bank Of England

Bartholomew Lane, EC2R 8AH

Founded in 1694, the Bank of England acts as the banker to the UK Government. Since the early nineteenth century it has occupied a prominent site bounded by Threadneedle Street, Prince's Street, Lothbury and Bartholomew Lane. Queen Elizabeth II was the first monarch to be featured on British bank notes – until 1960, Britannia had been the dominant character. Queen Elizabeth II visited the Bank of England in 1988 to open the Bank of England museum focusing on the history of the Bank. In 2012, Queen Elizabeth toured the gold vaults hidden

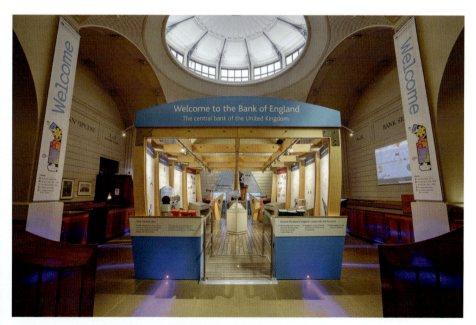

Entering the Bank of England Museum within the City of London.

deep underground to see 400,000 gold bars – an area which is out of bounds to the public!

Anyone visiting the museum does have an opportunity to try to lift a 13 kilo gold bar, carefully kept within a heavily protected case. Other exhibits on display include early bank notes, tally sticks and a 'gold' corridor. Special exhibitions are often held here such as Exploring London, People and Places, J.M.W. Turner and the Bank of England. There are various animated displays including William Pitt the Younger re-enacting a debate with his arch-rival

Try to lift a gold bar at the Bank of England.

Charles James Fox as well as interactive displays showing how to keep objects on an even keel.

Free to Visit

Opening hours
Monday to Friday 10am – 5pm

Nearest Underground
Bank 1 minute

www.bankofengland.co.uk

Barbican Centre

Silk Street, Barbican, EC2Y 8DS

The Barbican Centre represented the last massive development in the heart of the City following the destruction caused by the Second World War. When Queen Elizabeth II opened the Barbican in 1982, she described it as 'one of the modern wonders of the world'. It had taken a decade to build, and is named after a street that used to exist in the area before 1939. Built in a Brutalist architectural style, it is a complex of homes, apartments, restaurants, cafés, exhibition halls, theatre, cinema and library. The terrace blocks are built around a central lake and grassy squares. It can be confusing trying to find your way around the Barbican – the best way is to simply follow the yellow line until you reach a signpost pointing the way to your desired destination.

The theatre and cinema have a constantly changing programme of plays, films, concerts and screen talks.

The Barbican Centre opened by Queen Elizabeth in 1982.

Many of the major theatre companies such as the Royal Shakespeare Company have played at this venue.

Guided tours of the Barbican are sometimes available focusing on different aspects such as Architecture and Conservation.

Free to visit, but theatre and cinema productions require tickets to be purchased.

Opening hours
Monday to Saturday 9am – 11pm
Sunday 11am – 11pm

Nearest Underground
Barbican 6 minutes

www.barbican.org.uk/whats-on

Dans Le Noir

69-73 St John Street, Clerkenwell EC1M 4AN

Dining here is definitely both a challenge and an experience. There were rumours that Kate Middleton and Prince William dined here before their marriage, but it was difficult to prove simply because the entire dining experience is undertaken in pitch darkness! Mobile phones, cameras and luminous watches have to be locked away before entering the dining area.

Dans Le Noir has branches in Paris, Nantes, Bordeaux, Brussels, Luxembourg, Madrid, Barcelona and St Petersburg. Diners are encouraged to re-evaluate their sense of taste, while reclaiming all their senses, allowing them to have unexpected encounters. Everyone sits at large sharing tables, which means you have no idea who is sitting next to you. Menus are surprises, although you have to indicate before entering any dietary restrictions or allergies. All meals are served by blind or partially sighted waiting staff.

Pre-booking is essential.

Nearest Underground
Farringdon 6 minutes
Barbican 4 minutes

www.danslenoir.com

Guildhall

Gresham Street, EC2V 7HH

Visited by Queen Elizabeth II during her Silver Jubilee tour of the City of London, the Guildhall is the centre of local government for the area as it is the home of the City of London Corporation. There has been a building relating to local government on this site for over 800 years, and it includes the largest surviving medieval crypt in London. It is the oldest non-ecclesiastical stone building in the City. The ceiling has been totally destroyed twice – once during the Great Fire of London, and then during the London Blitz. It is quite a dramatic building, especially the seven foot high wooden effigies of Gog and Magog. These effigies play a leading role in the Lord Mayor's procession every November. According to legend, Gog and Magog were giants defeated by Brutus of Troy – the legendary founder of London – and were chained to the gates of the Guildhall. Also worth visiting is the Guildhall Art Gallery which contains many Pre-Raphaelite paintings and depictions of London over the centuries together with a changing programme of exhibitions such as Noël Coward art and Style and Wampum Stories from shells of North America. Don't miss the remains of Roman Londinium's amphitheatre in which 2,000 year old brickwork is bathed in light projections recreating the overall building design.

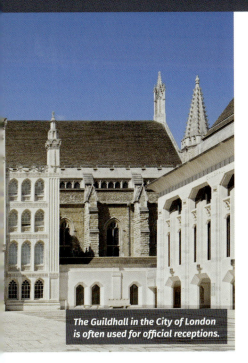

The Guildhall in the City of London is often used for official receptions.

Apart from its role in local government, it is often used for events sometimes attended by members of the royal family: for example the Princess Royal has been present several times, including signing the Book of Condolence to the victims of the London Bridge terror attack, while in 2020 she attended an official Awards Dinner at the Guildhall. Queen Elizabeth attended an official reception at the Guildhall to celebrate her ninetieth birthday while working members of the Royal Family attended a Platinum Jubilee lunch here following the service at St Paul's Cathedral in June 2022.

Entrance Free

Opening hours
Monday to Saturday 10am – 4.30pm
Sunday, March to September
      10am – 4.30pm

Nearest Underground
Bank 6 minutes
Mansion House 7 minutes

www.cityoflondon.gov.uk

Jubilee Walkway

City Loop, EC2R 8AH

The Jubilee Walkway began as part of Queen Elizabeth II's Silver Jubilee celebrations, with the first section around the City of London being opened by the Queen in 1977. The aim of the route was to connect London's key tourist attractions. In 2002, the route was renamed the Jubilee Walkway in honour of Queen Elizabeth's Golden Jubilee. There are now seven routes, totalling fifteen miles in total.

The City Loop covers two miles. Beginning at Bank and walking

Jubilee Walkway celebrating Queen Elizabeth II's Silver and Gold Jubilees.

anticlockwise, the route passes No 1 Poultry, The Guildhall, Guildhall Art Gallery, London Wall, Barbican, St Giles Church, Museum of London, Paternoster square, London Stock Exchange and St Paul's cathedral.

The Eastern Loop is five miles long, and starts at the Tate Modern on Bankside passing Shakespeare's Globe, the *Golden Hinde*, Southwark Cathedral, HMS *Belfast*, Tower Bridge, Tower of London, St Katherine's Docks, Monument, Bank of England, Royal Exchange, Mansion House and the Millennium Footbridge.

At six miles, the Western Loop is the longest of the Jubilee Walkway sections. Starting in Leicester square, it includes the National Gallery, Trafalgar Square, St James's Park, Westminster Abbey, London Eye, Oxo Tower, Tate Modern, St Paul's Cathedral, Lincoln's Inn Fields, Royal Opera House, Covent Garden and the London Transport Museum.

The three mile Camden Loop covers Chancery Lane, British Library, British Museum, and Coram's Fields.

The Jubilee Loop is the shortest at 1.7 miles. Starting in Trafalgar Square, it links Admiralty Arch, Pall Mall, Victoria Memorial, Buckingham Palace, Wellington Barracks, Parliament Square and St James's Park.

The exact itineraries can be found at www.jubileewalkway.org.uk. When following any of the routes, look for the jubilee discs embedded in the pavement.

Millennium Bridge

Bankside, SE1

Resplendent in bright pink on a sunny June day in 2000, Queen Elizabeth II opened the new Millennium Bridge across the Thames, stretching from just below St Paul's Cathedral to the Tate Modern on the South Bank. She was one of the first people to stroll across its elegant length. Two days later, the Millennium Bridge abruptly closed having earned itself the nickname of 'Wobbly Bridge'. It was two years before the public were allowed back.

The problem was that the bridge kept moving whenever people were walking across it. Some 80,000 people

The Millennium Bridge over the River Thames opened by Queen Elizabeth II in 2000.

crossed the Millennium Bridge on the first day, and there were around 2,000 people on the bridge at any one time. The bridge wobbled, swayed and began to noticeably twist. Eventually architects and engineers had to fit special shock absorbers at each end in order to contain the vertical movement.

The bridge cost £18.2m to construct, and was designed to align with the perfect vista of the south façade of St Paul's Cathedral.

Nearest Underground

Blackfriars 4 minutes
St Paul's 8 minutes
Southwark 9 minutes

Monument

Fish St Hill, London Bridge, EC3R 8AH

The Great Fire of London devastated the city. It began innocuously at a baker's house in Pudding Lane on 2 September 1666, and quickly spread out of control. Thousands of houses, hundreds of streets, public buildings, churches and even St Paul's Cathedral were destroyed, although only a few people died. King Charles II and his brother James (later James II) helped fight the fire, pulling down buildings to create fire breaks and carrying water from the Thames. The fire was not extinguished until 5 September.

King Charles II appointed Sir Christopher Wren to organise the

rebuilding, and was involved in many of the decisions on building style.

Built between 1671-1677, Monument commemorates the Great Fire and the rebuilding of London. A Doric column topped with an urn of flames, it is exactly 61 metres high (222 feet), marking the exact distance between the site where the fire began and the monument itself. Climbing the 311 steps to the top viewing gallery provides 360° panoramic views. Alternatively, watch live video images on the ground floor.

Entry fee.

Opening hours
April to September 9.30am – 6pm daily
9.30 am – 5.30 pm daily October/March
Closed 24 – 26 December

Nearest Underground
Monument 1 minute
Bank 5 minutes

www.themonument.info

Royal Philatelic Society

15 Abchurch Lane, Candlewick, EC4N 7BW

Founded in 1869, this is the oldest philatelic society in the world. As patron, Queen Elizabeth II opened its new headquarters in Abchurch Lane in 2019, marking the society's 150th anniversary.

Queen Elizabeth was a keen philatelist. The Royal Collection contains the largest and most complete collection of stamps from Great Britain and the Commonwealth. This royal hobby began when Prince Alfred – a younger son of Queen Victoria – began collecting stamps soon after the first stamps were launched. He later sold his collection to his brother, Edward VII. It was not until the reign of George V that new stamps were added to the collection. George V became a keen collector, especially of rare stamps, placing them in a series of red albums. His son, George VI, used blue albums and Elizabeth II introduced green albums. Queen Elizabeth often placed the collection on display, especially for charities.

The Royal Philatelic Society promotes the science and study of stamps, while maintaining unique stamp collections. It has a small museum containing items relating the development and design of stamps, examples of stamps and social items relating to stamp collecting.

Access is free, but must be pre arranged.

Opening hours
Monday to Friday10am – 4.00pm

Nearest Underground
Monument 2 minutes

www.rpsl.org.uk

Sadlers Wells

Roseberry Avenue, Clerkenwell, EC1R 4TN

The second oldest theatre in London, this is the sixth building on the site since it was founded in 1683. Over

Sadlers Wells theatre in Clerkenwell is the home of dance.

the years, it has hosted all types of theatrical entertainment including a singing duck! Sadlers Wells was the home of the Sadlers Wells Ballet Company founded by Ninette de Valois before it was renamed the Royal Ballet and moved to Covent Garden. The legendary ballerina Margot Fonteyn performed regularly at Sadlers Wells.

It is now the home of dance, and is a world leader in staging contemporary dance. There is a year round programme covering all types of dance including ballet, flamenco, tango and hip hop. Sadlers Wells aims to show that dance is available for everyone, surpassing all borders, cultures and languages. Sadlers Wells has several touring companies, which perform at venues across the UK as well as internationally.

The venue has attracted many royal visitors. Princess Margaret visited in 1956 to celebrate the twenty-fifth anniversary of Sadlers Wells reopening as a ballet venue. Both Princess Margaret and Princess Anne, the Princess Royal attended on various occasions. Not surprisingly, given Princess Diana's keen interest in dance, she visited several times to enjoy performances at Sadlers Wells, including a formal occasion when she wore a stunning Bruce Oldfield white satin and lace evening suit.

Opening hours
For performances only

Nearest Underground
Angel 5 minutes

www.sadlerswells.com

St Brides Church

Fleet Street EC4Y 8AU

One of the most distinctive churches in London, it is sometimes described as the Wedding Cake Church due to its 234ft tall tiered tower. It is said to have inspired the first tiered wedding cake, created by an eighteenth century local baker for his bride.

People have been worshipping on this site since Roman times. It was site of one of the most ancient, sacred wells in the city known as the Bride Well. The church is associated with St Bride (St Bridget of Kildare). The church was rebuilt following the Great Fire of London, and was largely gutted during the Blitz of WW2. It was rebuilt and reconstructed, then rededicated in the presence of Queen Elizabeth II and Prince Philip in 1957. Queen Elizabeth attended the 50th anniversary of that rededication in 2007.

Apart from providing a weekday ministry to people working in the area, St Brides has a long connection with journalists and the media from the days when Fleet Street was the home of newspapers. St Brides has a unique ministry to journalists and the media, with a Journalist's altar located in the church. Queen Consort Camilla is patron of the Guild of St Bride and has attended annual services commemorating journalists and other media personnel who have died on the front line, imprisoned, held hostage or are working in hostile situations.

Visitors can explore the church, see the Journalists altar, Roman remains and other historical artefacts as well as a memorial to Polly Nichols, first victim of Jack the Ripper, who was married here in 1864.

Opening hours
Monday-Friday: 8am - 5pm
Saturday: 10am – 3.30pm
Sunday: 10am – 6.30 pm

Nearest Underground
St Pauls 5 minutes
Blackfriars 6 minutes

www.stbrides.com

St Paul's Cathedral

St Paul's Churchyard, EC4M 8AD

The sight of Charles and Diana walking down the steps of St Paul's following their wedding has become one of the most iconic Royal images of the twentieth century. The cathedral had been chosen as the venue because it was the only one large enough to hold the sheer number of invited guests. It was the first wedding of an heir to the throne held at this cathedral for 480 years.

It was not the first time that St Paul's had become a British icon. During the Second World War, it became a symbol of resistance due to an amazing photograph showing fires blazing during the blitz while St Paul's stands clearly visible through the smoke and destruction. The Prime Minister, Winston Churchill, stated that St Paul's 'must be saved at all costs.' When victory came, thousands visited it as part of the celebrations.

It has been the focus of many celebrations including hosting National Services of Thanksgiving on the occasion of Queen Elizabeth's Silver, Gold, Diamond and Platinum Jubilees, as well as Queen Victoria's Diamond Jubilee. In October 2022, the Princess Royal attended the Annual National Service for Seafarers.

Other events include the funeral of Sir Winston Churchill, which was

The setting of numerous Royal events including the wedding of Prince Charles and Diana Spencer, St Paul's Cathedral is an iconic building.

attended by royalty, and a service celebrating the opening of the 2012 Paralympic Games, complete with a game of wheelchair basketball under the Dome. It featured in the 1960s film *Mary Poppins* with the memorable 'Feed the Birds' song filmed on the steps of St Pauls.

The Cathedral has had an incredibly chequered past. There has been a church on this site since the seventh century, and it has been rebuilt and destroyed several times, especially when it was burned to the ground during the Great Fire of London. Sir Christopher Wren's impressive baroque church with its massive dome dates from the seventeenth century. The Dome is one of the largest in the world, and comprises three distinct domes – the familiar outer shell, a brick cone providing the strength to support the stone lantern and an inner painted dome. Visitors can visit the Whispering Gallery, the Stone Gallery and the Golden Gallery – but it does involve a tremendous amount of steps. There are no lifts, with the Golden Gallery involving 528 steps from the base of the cathedral. Sufficient to say that the views from the top are spectacular!

The Crypt contains the tombs of Lord Nelson, Lord Wellington and Sir Christopher Wren as well as memorials to famous people like Alexander Fleming, who discovered penicillin. The American Memorial Chapel was opened by President Eisenhower and dedicated to the memory of the Americans stationed in London during the Second World War.

Admission fees are payable to enter the Cathedral outside service times. Guided tours are available throughout the day at no extra cost, but places have to be booked on arrival. Introductory talks are frequently held.

Opening hours
Monday to Saturday for sightseeing
    8.30am – 4.30pm
Monday to Saturday Dome Galleries
    9.30am – 4.30pm
Sunday open for worship only

Nearest Underground
St Paul's 2 minutes
Mansion House 5 minutes

www.stpauls.co.uk

Sushisamba
Heron Tower, 110 Bishopsgate, EC2N 4AY

According to Princess Eugenie's Pinterest account, this is one of her favourite dining destinations, although she does offer a word of warning, commenting, 'Get in the lift and look out across London. Careful though, as it goes fast and high, so makes you feel a little wobbly.'

SushiSamba specialises in Japanese, Brazilian and Peruvian cuisine. Views are certainly spectacular since it is located on the highest dining terrace in Europe. Apart from enjoying a meal here, guests can relax by the fire pit on the iconic tree tower, have fun in the 39th Bar to music played by DJ's and drink handcrafted cocktails.

Opening hours
Sunday to Monday: 11.30am – 1am
Tuesday to Wednesday: 11.30am – 2am
Thursday to Saturday: 11.30am – 3am

Nearest Underground
Liverpool Street 5 minutes

www.sushisamba.com

Temple Bar

Paternoster Row, EC4M 7DX

Traffic into the City of London swerves around a massive pedestal crowned by a dramatic, eye-catching sculpture of a dragon seemingly swooping down on people below. It also marks an important spot in royal links with the area since this used to be a major gateway into the City of London. Whenever the monarch ceremonially arrives in the City, the carriage stops at this point. The Lord Mayor approaches and offers the Pearl Sword as a sign of loyalty. The monarch touches it, then returns it. This ceremony reflects the fact that the office of Lord Mayor of London was created by the sovereign hundreds of years ago – the office, title and dignity of Lord Mayor comes directly from the monarch. The involvement of the Pearl Sword is believed to date from 1588, when

The griffin on guard at the entrance to the City of London.

Queen Elizabeth I was on a procession through the area, celebrating the defeat of the Spanish Armada. At Temple Bar, the Lord Mayor of London presented her with the keys of the City. In return she gave him a jewelled sword.

The Lord Mayor of London is one of the members of the Accession Council who meet to proclaim a new sovereign's right to the throne. During the Coronation ceremony, the Lord Mayor stands close to the throne. The Livery Companies of the City of London also play a part in the event as the Glovers provide gloves, and the Girdlers a belt and a stole. The Chandlers' Company provide beeswax candles for important royal events such as the Coronation, royal funerals and royal weddings such as that of Prince Charles and Diana Spencer. Various members of the Royal Family have held various positions within the Livery Companies: for example the Princess Royal is perpetual master of the Saddlers' Company and has served as Master of eight other livery companies.

Nearest Underground

Blackfriars 10 minutes
Temple 18 minutes

www.cityoflondon.gov.uk

Tower Of London

Tower Hill, EC3N 4AB

For nearly 1,000 years, the Tower of London has dominated the north bank of the River Thames on the edge of the city of London. It was the first stone castle of its kind built in Britain, with an imposing keep designed to stamp the authority of William the Conqueror upon his new Saxon subjects. Over the next 600 years, the fortress was steadily expanded, adding new buildings and new fortifications, including royal quarters modernised to house Ann Boleyn, just before her coronation as Henry VIII's new queen.

Within months, the Tower became her prison, and ultimately the site of her execution. A similar fate faced Henry's fifth wife, Katherine Howard, likewise Lady Jane Grey, the nine days queen. Even Queen Elizabeth I, while still a princess, found herself imprisoned here.

Until late in the seventeenth century, it was customary for monarchs to stay at the Tower in the royal apartments immediately before their coronation, before processing down to Westminster Abbey through the city on their coronation day. Charles II was the last king to make such a journey.

Panoramic view of the Tower of London.

Marking the spot where Tudor queens were executed.

The Tower of London remains a royal palace and fortress, housing the most important items of the royal regalia – the Crown Jewels. Located in the Jewel House, these are the most visited objects in Britain. The Crown Jewels are not just for display as they are still used. The Imperial State Crown is worn by the monarch at the State Opening of Parliament, and is taken there in secret by Yeoman Warders using a specially created case to hold the crown in place. The Imperial State Crown, along with the Sovereign's Sceptre and Orb were

Standing guard within the Tower of London.

placed on the Queen Elizabeth's coffin for the Lying in State at Westminster Hall and the funeral service at Westminster Abbey.

The royal regalia will be used in the coronation of King Charles III, and in turn that of his heir, William, Prince of Wales when he inherits the crown. By far the most important item is St Edward's Crown, which is only used at the moment of crowning itself. Also on display are crowns worn by various royal consorts, such as Queen Elizabeth the Queen Mother's crown, together with the Coronation robes worn by Queen Elizabeth II.

There have been unsuccessful attempts to steal the Crown Jewels, most notably by Colonel Blood in 1671.

In March 1994, Queen Elizabeth II opened a new Crown Jewels display within the Waterloo Block of the Tower of London. The exhibition was refurbished in 2012, enabling you to stand just a few centimetres from the most valuable and prestigious jewels in the world. On display are a variety of crowns worn by kings and queens over the centuries, the royal regalia, coronation robes, gold plate and goblets. In 2020, Prince Charles' Investiture Coronet was added to the

The majestic White Tower at the heart of the Tower of London.

display for the first time, joining the coronets of two previous Princes of Wales.

On the King's birthday and other royal occasions, a royal gun salute is fired at the Gun Park on the Wharf. There is no public access to the Wharf during the set up and duration of the gun salute, although it can be viewed on Tower Hill or, for ticket holders only, within the Tower itself. The guns are fired by the Royal Artillery and usually involve 62 rounds.

Members of the Royal Family have visited the Tower on numerous occasions. In 2014, Queen Elizabeth II, the Duke and Duchess of Cambridge (now Prince & Princess of Wales) and Prince Harry came to view the thousands of ceramic poppies placed around the tower and falling down the walls in tribute to the soldiers who died during the First World War. Prince Harry launched the UK Invictus Games in a ceremony attended by ninety athletes at the Tower in 2017. In February 2020,

Traitors' Gate – the traditional entrance from the river used to bring Henry VIII's wives to their execution.

King Charles III marked the 535th anniversary of the creation of the Yeoman Warders at the Tower, and was shown the Crown Jewels.

The Yeomen Warders take part in many royal occasions such as during the Funeral of Queen Elizabeth II and coronation of King Charles III.

Exploring the Tower of London provides lots of royal experiences. See Traitors Gate through which Anne Boleyn and Katherine Howard passed to meet their eventual fate on Tower Green, discover the Chapel of St Peter Ad Vincula where the Queens lie buried, and the story of the Princes in the Tower, whose fate is unknown but who may well have been murdered.

Take a look too at the amazing horse armoury, and armour once worn by medieval kings, or discover an amazing dragon sculpture.

The infamous ravens are irresistible and can be found anywhere within the Tower, from the top of the White Tower to sitting on the cannons. Beware your food – they have been known to steal it! One of the ravens has the unusual name of Jubilee 2. In 2012, the Tower of London decided they would give Queen Elizabeth a raven as a present to commemorate her Diamond Jubilee. It would naturally stay at the Tower as one of the Tower ravens. Shortly after presenting the bird, the Ravenmaster went to America on holiday. On arrival he was greeted by a desperate phone call announcing that a fox had killed

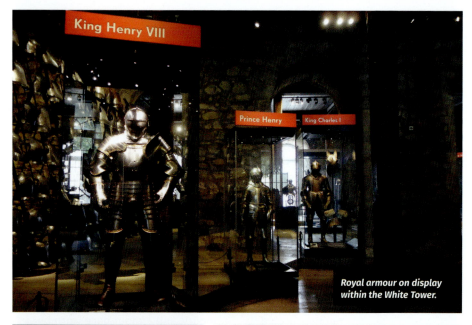

Royal armour on display within the White Tower.

One of the legendary Tower ravens perching on a historic gun.

Dragon sculpture created out of armour in the White Tower.

Jubilee. Fortunately a replacement was quickly found and named Jubilee 2.

Head into the White Tower and discover the secrets of warfare waged by so many royal princes over the years, where you can attempt to fire a cannon, joust and use a long bow.

Pre-booking tickets is recommended, as the Tower of London is extremely popular. The Yeomen Warders provide free guided tours of the main areas of the Tower on a regular basis throughout the day, and there are also free talks about the ravens from one of the Ravenmaster's team.

A Yeomen Warder at the Tower of London.

Opening hours
Hours vary according to season
Tuesday to Saturday 9am – 5.30pm
Sunday and Monday 10am – 5.30pm

Nearest Underground
Tower Hill 2 minutes

www.hrp.org.uk/tower-of-london

Tower Bridge

Tower Bridge Road, SE1 2UP

With towers rising majestically 143 feet high, Tower Bridge is one of the most iconic sights of London. Built in Victorian gothic style, it was opened by the Prince of Wales (later Edward VII) on behalf of Queen Victoria in 1894. In 2010, his descendent Queen Elizabeth II came to visit. Before strolling across the central part of the bridge, she visited the Tower Bridge exhibition and toured the high level walkways, meeting people who work on the River Thames.

Stunning panoramic views can be enjoyed from the high-level walkways, which were only reopened to the public in 1982. Originally these walkways were uncovered and open to the elements. They did not remain in use for very long, being closed in 1910 as the walkways had become a haunt for pickpockets and prostitutes, as well as being hard to reach. Not many people wanted to climb the 206 steps. Nowadays, it is much more comfortable. A lift is available to take visitors to the top of the towers, and the walkways

Tower Bridge offers panoramic views from the high-level walkways reopened by Queen Elizabeth II.

are now covered by glass. You can even walk across a glass floor to see the river flowing far below.

At ground level, visitors can explore the Victorian engine rooms to see how the bridge is raised. Ships have right of way at all times – even US President Clinton's motorcade had to wait twenty minutes in 1997 as the Thames Barge *Gladys* had priority. The two sides of the bridge are lifted up to allow boats to pass underneath. This is now done remotely by computer, and the Tower Bridge website contains details as to when the bridge is scheduled to be raised. On average, Tower Bridge is raised at least three times daily to allow tall ships to pass.

A warning bell is sounded when the bridge is about to be raised, giving people time to get clear. On one memorable occasion in 1952, the bridge began to rise with a London double-decker bus driven by Albert Gunter still crossing it – he took the decision to speed up and managed to leap from one side to the other as it rose.

Originally painted chocolate brown, the Bridge changed colour in 1977 to red, white and blue in honour of Queen Elizabeth's silver jubilee. Some years later in 1982 following a renovation project, it changed colour again to blue and white. The bridge is constructed from Cornish granite, Portland Stone and steel and took eight years to build.

Walking over the bridge is free of charge as it is a public highway. Access to the High Walkway and exhibition area requires payment. Behind the

scenes guided tours require pre-booking

Opening hours
High Walkway and exhibition 9.30am – 5pm daily
Closed 24 – 26 December

Nearest Underground
Tower Hill 7 minutes

DLR station
Tower Gateway 7 minutes

By river
St Katherine's Pier 1 minute
Tower Pier North bank 9 minutes

www.towerbridge.org.uk

Wilton's Music Hall, a Victorian gem, opened by King Charles III.

Wilton's Music Hall

1 Graces Alley, E1 8JB

Tucked away in an alley close to the Tower of London and St Katherine's Dock is a Victorian gem, supported by King Charles III. Parts of the building date back to the 1690s as areas now used as a box office, bars, offices and rehearsal space were once houses, shops and a pub providing entertainment for local people. In 1853 John Wilton started trading on the site, and by 1859 had combined several buildings to provide the first ever music hall. His aim was to provide West End glamour, comfort and entertainment for East End working people. It became a massive success, quickly followed by other entrepreneurs

The restored interior of London's first ever Victorian music hall.

across the country setting up their own music halls. Some of the performers at Wilton's Music became household names familiar nationwide. Among those performers were people like Champagne Charlie, and their songs in the 1860s led them to become the first music hall stars to perform for royalty. Changing times led to the decline of the music hall, and Wilton's eventually became a Methodist Mission hall. By the end of the twentieth century, the building lay derelict.

As Patron of Wilton's Music Hall, King Charles III made his first visit to the derelict building in 2006, viewing plans for restoration. Ten years later, in 2016, he came back to reopen Wilton's Music Hall. During the opening ceremony, local school children sang a programme of music hall songs followed by a short variety performance on the newly restored music hall stage. A document commemorating the visit was framed and hung in the John Wilton Room.

There is a constantly changing programme of music and dance held at the music hall on a regular basis, together with restaurants and cocktails bars open to the public. You can book a guided tour around the building, discovering its unique history and stories of the performers and people associated with it.

Opening hours
Monday – Friday 11am – 6pm
Closed weekends

Nearest DLR
Tower Gateway 7 minutes

Nearest Underground
Aldgate East 9 minutes
Tower Hill 11 minutes

www.wiltons.org.uk

SOUTH LONDON

Battersea Park

Albert Bridge Road, Wandsworth, SW11 4NJ

Celebrating their first Christmas together in 2016, Prince Harry and Meghan Markle were spotted buying a Christmas tree at the Pine and Needles Christmas Store in Battersea Park. Fronting onto the Thames itself with a riverside promenade, the park stretches between Chelsea Bridge and Albert Bridge. Originally created in the Victorian period, it covers 200 acres of land and was reopened by Prince Philip in 2004 following a major refurbishment. The extensive lawns and beautiful lake make it a great place to relax or go for a stroll. There are good sports facilities as well as a children's play area and zoo. An unusual feature is the large Peace Pagoda, which has been a local landmark for over 20 years. This Buddhist Temple is open to the public, and is a great place for meditation. Inside are four large gilded bronze statues of the Buddha.

Don't forget to take a stroll over the adjacent Albert Bridge. The bridge was built at the suggestion of Prince Albert, Queen Victoria's consort and was named in his honour. It has an unusual architectural style combining concrete pillars and suspension cables. It is very photogenic, especially at night when it is illuminated by over 4,000 lights to ensure no boats collide with it.

Take a look at the unusual notice at the entrance to the bridge. The signs warn troops to break step when crossing the bridge – this refers to soldiers who were based at Chelsea Barracks. They were requested to stop marching in rhythm as they passed over as it made the bridge vibrate! So strong was the vibration, that it became nicknamed the Trembling Lady.

Opening hours
8am – dusk daily

Nearest Underground
Vauxhall 34 minutes

Nearest Train
Battersea Park 1 minute

www.batterseapark.org

British Film Theatre

South Bank, SE1 8XT

This was one of the locations visited by Queen Elizabeth during her 2012 Jubilee tour of the area. Many years earlier, Charles and Diana attended events here.

The British Film Theatre is a four-screen cinema complex, showing a range of classic and contemporary films, and director and actor retrospectives. There is a contemporary art gallery on site dedicated to the moving image. Stop off and browse the extensive second-hand book stalls outside and along the river bank – a popular feature of this area.

Opening hours
11am – 11pm daily
Friday and Saturday11am – 11.30pm

Nearest Underground
Waterloo 4 minutes

www.bfi.org.uk

Dulwich Picture Gallery

Gallery Road, SE21 7AD

King Charles III, Queen Consort Camilla and the Princess of Wales visited Dulwich Picture Gallery to see work carried out by the Prince's Foundation for Children and the Arts. The royal trio got creative with silk printing – ironing transfer onto silk.

Dulwich Picture Gallery contains a superb collection of old master paintings, regarded as one of the best in the world. In 1790, Sir Francis Bourgeois was commissioned to create a royal art collection for the King of Poland. Unfortunately, the king abdicated before he could take possession of the artworks. Sir Francis managed to sell some art elsewhere, but was still left with a massive collection. He eventually gave it to Dulwich College with the stipulation that the paintings should be available

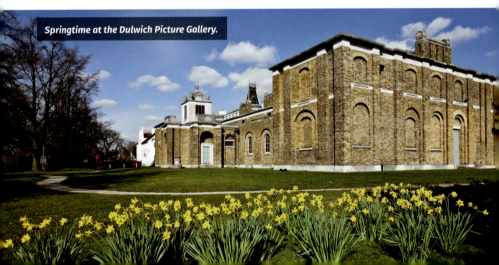
Springtime at the Dulwich Picture Gallery.

Art masterpieces on view in the Dulwich Picture Gallery.

Old Master art at the Dulwich Picture Gallery.

for 'inspection of the public'. Opening to the public in 1811, it was the first ever purpose-built public art gallery providing the opportunity to see masterpieces by artists like Rembrandt, Gainsborough, Poussin, Watteau and Canaletto. Since then the collection has increased steadily. Many special exhibitions are held here such as British Surrealism, together with creative courses, talks and lectures.

There are free gallery guided tours held at 3pm every Saturday and Sunday.

Entrance charge

Opening hours
Tuesday – Sunday 10am – 5.00pm
Closed Mondays (except Bank Holidays)
Christ's Chapel Tuesday 1.30pm – 3.30pm

Nearest Train
West Dulwich and North Dulwich
    10 minutes

Nearest Underground
Brixton then a P4 Bus to the Gallery

www.dulwichpicturegallery.org.uk

The Golden Hinde

St Mary Overie's Dock, Cathedral Street, SE1 9DE

Moored on the South Bank is an unusual vessel linked to the Tudor Queen Elizabeth I. *The Golden Hinde* is an exact replica of Sir Francis Drake's famous vessel in which he became the first English captain to circumnavigate

The Golden Hinde, *an exact replica of Sir Francis Drake's famous ship in which he circumnavigated the world.*

the world. On his return, laden with treasure (mostly stolen *en route* as a result of his privateering activities), he was knighted by Queen Elizabeth I. She had been an investor in his long voyage and took a share of the proceeds.

This replica was hand-built using traditional techniques and materials, including the creation of all the furnishings, the Hinde figurehead and the twenty-two cannons carried on board. Launched in 1973, it has become a major tourist attraction and educational facility as well as being a sea going vessel.

Visitors can explore every part of the ship, talking to staff re-enacting the roles of the sailors who crewed her over 400 years ago. Discover the stories of Drake's famous voyage, and join the crew to experience life on board.

Entrance charge.

Opening hours
10.00am – 6.00pm (closing at 5pm in winter) daily

Nearest Underground
London Bridge 6 minutes
Borough 10 minutes

By river
London Bridge City Pier 6 minutes
Bankside Pier 6 minutes

www.goldenhinde.co.uk

HMS Belfast
The Queen's Walk, SE1 2JH

Just like the Tardis, HMS *Belfast* is bigger on the inside than she outwardly seems. With nine separate decks, places like the boiler room and engine room are fifteen feet below sea level. One of only three remaining ships from the D-Day bombardment fleet, she is permanently moored in the Thames. HMS *Belfast* also saw action in the North Sea, fighting on the arctic convoys to Russia. In 2010, new masts were dedicated in an event attended by Prince Philip and officials from the Russian Government. HMS *Belfast* is often used as a venue for special events. In 2007, she hosted the naming ceremony for the lighthouse tender THV *Galatea*, attended by Queen Elizabeth and Prince Philip.

A long walkway leads out into the Thames providing access to HMS

The iconic Second World War cruiser, HMS Belfast, moored on the Thames.

Belfast. Once on board, you can explore all nine decks including the mess decks, sick bay, gun direction platform, galley, sailors quarters, captain's cabin, and climb up to the flag deck. There are several challenging hands-on activities available including helping to recover a downed plane, and learning how to navigate.

Entrance charge.

Opening hours
10am – 6pm daily

Nearest Underground
London Bridge 7 minutes
Tower Hill 16 minutes

www.iwm.org.uk/visits/hms-belfast

Horniman Museum

100 London Road, Forest Hill, SE23 3PG

A museum tucked away in south London where unusual surprises lie in store. On display are various royal items, including a piano used by Queen Victoria, a Horniman's Tea Caddy showing Edward VII and Queen Alexandra enjoying a cup of tea, a Nigerian statue of Queen Victoria and some unique Nigerian rod puppets showing Princess Diana in a white wedding dress with veil, holding a bouquet of bright red and yellow flowers.

Explore the World Gallery containing over 3,000 items from around the world, many of which can be touched and handled. Among the exhibits are Tuareg metalwork, aromatic herbs used by Bhutanese ritual healers, a Lagos market and a totem pole. Stroll through sixteen acres of gardens and an area devoted to sheep, goats, alpacas and other animals plus an aquarium and butterfly house.

Free entry. Exhibitions and special events may incur a charge.

Opening hours
7.15am – sunset Grounds daily
10am – 5.30pm World Gallery museum daily

Nearest Train
Forest Hill 8 minutes

www.horniman.ac.uk

Imperial War Museum

Lambeth Road, SE1 6HZ

The vast archives held at the Imperial War Museum hold many secrets, as the Princess of Wales discovered during a surprise visit in 2018. Tucked away in the archives were letters written by her great grandmother's three brothers, all of whom fought and died during the First World War. One of the sons, Maurice, wrote home asking for nightlights and pencils to be sent to him. The Princess was shown around the First World War Galleries during her visit.

Her husband, the Prince of Wales, is President of the Imperial War Museum

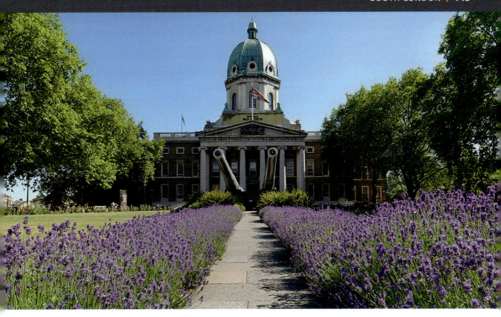

Approaching the entrance to the Imperial War Museum London.

Foundation. During his visit in 2017, he explored new Second World War galleries including the Holocaust space setting personal stories of the Holocaust within the context of the war, and met numerous veterans.

The Imperial War Museum is more than a military history museum. It tells the story of a world at war, of life in the trenches, the events surrounding the fall of the Berlin Wall and the Cold War as well as highlighting issues relating to peace and security since 1945. There are many unexpected items to see, some of which are eye-catching or very sad such as the trunk belonging to Leonard and Clara Cohen. They had sent their daughters to safety in the UK, and had sent their own belongings on ahead to South America. Sadly, before they could board a ship to take them to safety, they were arrested and sent to Auschwitz where they died. Their daughters received the trunks after the war ended. Other items on display include wooden horse trainers, part of the Dambusters Bar and an improvised sofa made by troops serving in Afghanistan.

Admission is free.

Opening hours
10am – 6pm daily
Closed 24 – 26 December

Nearest Underground
Lambeth North 10 minutes
Elephant and Castle 12 minutes

www.iwm.org.uk

Jubilee Gardens

The Queen's Walk, South Bank, SE1 7PB

This South Bank park was first developed to mark Queen Elizabeth II Silver Jubilee in 1977. It underwent a refurbishment in 2012, just in time for the Diamond Jubilee celebrations during which Queen Elizabeth unveiled a plaque on site. The newly landscaped parkland includes ninety-seven trees, new pathways, flowerbeds and a small children's adventure playground. There are great views of the Houses of Parliament, Big Ben and boats sailing along the river. Each December it is the setting for a fairy-tale Christmas market.

Admission free.

Opening hours
24 hours a day, although the adventure playground closes at dusk.

Nearest Underground
Waterloo 5 minutes
Westminster 7 minutes

www.jubileegardens.org.uk

London Bridge Station

20 Stainer Street, SE1 9RL

The fourth busiest station in London, millions of travellers pass through it *en route* to destinations across southeast England, including Gatwick Airport. The Prince of Wales opened the revamped station following a £7bn transformation, creating a street level station big enough to lay down the nearby Shard building on the floor. To reach the station, he travelled on a Thameslink train. His arrival marked not just the transformation of the station, but also the end of his paternity leave following the birth of Prince Louis. During his visit, the Prince signed the visitors' book, viewed a model of the station and met staff and apprentices involved in the transformation.

Opening hours
Monday to Saturday 4am – 1am
Sunday 6am – 1am

Nearest Underground
London Bridge 1 minute

www.networkrail.couk/passengers/our-stations/londonbridge

London Eye

The Queen's Walk, South Bank, SE1 7PB

If you have a head for heights, this is definitely one of the best ways to view London. At 443 feet tall, with a diameter of 394 feet, it is Europe's tallest observation wheel and stands on a platform erected just over the Thames. It was originally intended as a temporary structure to mark the Millennium – it proved so popular that it stayed.

Among the most well-known passengers are the Prince & Princess of Wales, Prince Harry. The trio took a ride on the wheel in 2016 in support of the Heads Together initiative on World

The London Eye on the South Bank overlooking the River Thames.

Mental Health Day. They were joined on the ride by some of the people who had been sharing their mental health experiences at a reception in nearby County Hall.

The London Eye caught the attention of Princess Eugenie who pinned images of it on her Instagram site while highlighting her favourite iconic London landmarks. She wrote admiringly 'the London Eye offers a spectacular view of the great city.'

The wheel never stops turning, even to let passengers on or off. The wheel rotates at just 26 cms/10 inches per second allowing passengers to enter and leave the pods at ground level. One revolution of the wheel takes 30 minutes and you can walk around or sit down during the ride. Special experiences can be booked such as champagne receptions.

Tickets should be pre-booked as it is very popular. You can buy a combined ticket with linked attractions such as Madame Tussauds and the Sealife London Aquarium.

Opening hours
10am daily, closing between 6pm and 8.30pm depending on season.

Nearest Underground
Waterloo 5 minutes
Westminster 7 minutes

www.londoneye.com

National Theatre

Upper Ground, SE1 9PX

In March 2020, the National Theatre was the venue for one of the Duchess of Sussex's last royal activities. For many years, The Queen was patron of the National Theatre, before passing on the patronage to Meghan Markle, Duchess of Sussex in 2019. Meghan visited the National Theatre in January 2020, just hours before announcing that she and Prince Harry were standing down as senior royals. She then made a further low-key visit in March to tour the theatre and visit its immersive storytelling studio in one of her final visits as a working royal. Queen Consort Camilla is now the royal patron and has taken part in various activities at the theatre.

The National Theatre is one of the most well-known performing arts venues. It opened in 1963 with a production of *Hamlet* directed by the legendary Laurence Olivier. One of its most popular productions was *War Horse* by Michael Morpurgo which opened to rave reviews in 2007, and was eventually turned into a film premiered in front of the Prince & Princess of Wales. As a play, it enjoyed a massive eight-year run at the National Theatre.

The National Theatre hosts a continually changing programme of productions within its complex, which includes the Olivier Theatre and the Lyttelton Theatre, plus restaurants and bars.

Nearest Underground
Waterloo 5 minutes
Embankment 11 minutes

The National Theatre is a major performing arts venue.

The Oval

Kennington, SE11 5SS

Owned by the Prince of Wales' Duchy of Cornwall, the Oval is the home of Surrey County Cricket Club, one of the oldest cricket clubs in the country. International cricket matches have been held here since 1880 and the legendary Ashes were born here two years later. Back in 2013, Prince Charles visited to inspect the new pavilion, which now houses a replica Ashes Urn. He visited the Oval again in 2017 to celebrate the launch of the ICC Champions Trophy and watched a tournament involving local primary schools.

Another royal visitor was definitely in a celebratory mood when he came in May 2019. Just after the birth of his son, Prince Harry opened the ICC Cricket World Cup match – the first to be held in England since 1975.

It is not just cricket that has made sporting history at the Oval – it was the site of the first international football match in 1870, the first FA Cup Final, and the first Rugby Union Cup Fixture.

Exploring the Oval is possible via behind the scenes tours of the grounds, lasting around ninety minutes. During the tour you explore the grounds, visit the pavilions, see the historic clock and go through the famous Bradman doors, discover the stories of cricketing legends, see archive material and visit the players' changing rooms and function rooms.

Tours must be pre-booked.

Nearest Underground
Oval 2 minutes
Vauxhall 10 minutes

www.kiaoval.com

Owned by the Prince of Wales, the Oval is an iconic cricketing venue.

Prince Albert Pub

85 Albert Bridge Road, Battersea, SW11 4PF

Football fan Prince William turned up at the Prince Albert pub, Battersea to watch the Euro2020 qualifying match between England and the Czech Republic, accompanied by former England captain Frank Lampard. It was not all fun however, as his visit was linked to his work at The Royal Foundation and his patronage of the Football Association. Also present were fans who had accessed the services of mental health charities. The Prince's visit was aimed to encourage people to 'feel as comfortable talking about their mental health as they do talking about football in the pub.'

The venue was well chosen. Dating back to 1866, it is now a gastropub providing a good selection of real ales, open fires and a beer garden, located close to Battersea Park.

Nearest Underground
Vauxhall 34 minutes

Nearest Train
Battersea Park 1 minute

www.theprincealbertbattersea.co.uk

Restaurant Story

199 Tooley Street, SE1 2JX

Princess Beatrice showed she was quick to find good restaurants because less than five months after she ate here it was awarded a Michelin star.

Built on the site of a former toilet block in Tooley Street, Restaurant Story is definitely unusual. It is a stylish venue with understated décor complete with an open kitchen so you can watch the cooks at work; the food is imaginative and experimental. The menu includes classic story dishes such as the Three Bears Porridge – a trio of hot oat bowls, one too sweet, one too salty and one just right. Another signature dish is Bread and Dripping in which an edible beef dripping candle is lit at the table, and served with bread to mop up the melted 'wax'. Every dish is designed to invoke memories via story lines or seasonally inspired creations.

Opening hours
Mondays 6.30pm – 9pm
Tuesday to Saturday 12 midday – 2pm,
	6.30pm – 9pm
Closed Sundays

Nearest Underground
London Bridge 10 minutes
Bermondsey 15 minutes

www.restaurantstory.co.uk

Richmond Park

Richmond, TW10 5HS

At 2,500 acres, Richmond Park is the biggest of all the royal parks in London. It is also a national nature reserve. This is a great place for walking and relaxing due to the mix of woodland gardens, ancient trees, grassy open spaces and meadows. Herds of fallow deer and red deer roam through the parkland. The Isabella Plantation woodland garden is particularly stunning.

The royal connections go back a long way. The area was known as the manor of Sheen when visited by medieval kings like Edward I. It became known as Richmond Park during the reign of Henry VIII. According to legend King Henry's Mound is where he saw a rocket fired from the Tower of London to signal the execution of Anne Boleyn. While a nice story, it is a legend since he was in Wiltshire at the time. Climbing to the top of the mound offers brilliant panoramic views as far away as St Paul's Cathedral. Both Henry VIII and Elizabeth I were frequent visitors to Richmond Park as it was one of their favourite hunting grounds. Elizabeth I died at Richmond Palace in 1603. Nothing is now left of that palace apart from the gatehouse.

White Lodge was once a royal residence. Built by George II and Queen Caroline, it was popular with George III and Queen Charlotte. Queen Victoria and Prince Albert stayed here in 1858, when the Queen painted scenes in her garden. White Lodge was the birthplace of Edward VIII – the uncle of Queen Elizabeth II. He reigned for only a few months, preferring to abdicate before his coronation so as to wed his beloved Mrs Simpson.

Queen Elizabeth stayed at White Lodge as a baby, as Queen Mary gave the house to her parents, hoping they would enjoy it as much as she had. Unfortunately, lack of privacy made them give up the house in 1927, a year after Queen Elizabeth's birth.

White Lodge is not open to the public. It is now the home of the Royal Ballet School, training young dancers.

During the 2012 Diamond Jubilee celebrations, Queen Elizabeth returned to explore the park as part of a wildlife event. She inaugurated the Diamond Jubilee pond, and enjoyed performances by the Chapel Royal choir and the Royal Ballet School.

Free entry

Opening hours
24 hours daily

Nearest Underground
Richmond 49 minutes

www.royalparks.org.uk/parks/
richmond-park

Royal Botanic Gardens

Kew Gardens, Kew, Richmond, TW9 3AE

Created out of two royal estates in the 1759 by Princess Augusta, the Royal Botanic Gardens have been open to the public since 1840. A beautiful arboretum of 14,000 trees, a Capability Brown designed Rhododendron dell, a giant badger sett and over 50,000 plants have resulted in these gardens being declared a UNESCO world heritage site.

The royal connections have been continued over the years. King Charles

Royal Botanic Gardens, Kew showing the Glasshouse opened by the Diana, Princess of Wales.

III visited the Millennium Seed Bank to donate wild flower seeds from his Highgrove Estate, while in 2017 he visited the Great Broad Walk borders. Queen Elizabeth II visited Kew on many occasions since her first official visit in 1959, including a visit to celebrate Kew's 250th anniversary in 2009.

In 1987, Diana, Princess of Wales opened the massive central Glasshouse covering 4,500 sq. metres of growing space. Walking through the Glasshouse, you pass through 10 different climatic zones, discovering cacti, carnivorous plants, orchids and bromeliads – as well as fish and Chinese water dragons. Exploring Kew you are truly travelling around the world in just one site!

Another popular part of the site is the Treetop Walkway where you can walk through the tops of the trees, seeing the Gardens from above.

Not to be missed is the Great Pagoda, which has been refurbished and re-opened as a public attraction. You do need some stamina to climb it, as it is 253 steps to the top but once there the views are spectacular. To provide some entertainment while you climb, there are displays explaining how it was built and how the royal family used it. Also worth visiting is

Queen Charlotte's cottage – a small rustic retreat tucked away within the grounds.

Kew Palace is the smallest of all the royal palaces, a very intimate building used primarily by eighteenth century royalty, especially King George III, who suffered from mental illness. In 2006, Queen Elizabeth II celebrated her eightieth birthday here with a family dinner party. Adjacent to Kew Palace are the Georgian Royal Kitchens, which remain unchanged from when they were last used, over 200 years ago. The kitchen gardens are fun to visit.

At Christmas time, Kew Gardens takes on a magical aspect as it is transformed by extensive illuminations, including cascading waterfalls of light around the grounds.

Entry to the Palace is included within the overall ticket to Kew Gardens. An additional fee is required to visit the interior of the Great Pagoda.

Opening hours
10am – 6.30pm daily

Nearest Underground
Kew Gardens 5 minutes

www.kew.org

Kew Palace, the most intimate of all the royal palaces.

Royal Festival Hall

Southbank Centre, SE1 8XX

Back in 1951, the South Bank, including the Royal Festival Hall, was the setting of the Festival of Britain celebrating art, science, music, industry and design. Princess Elizabeth and Prince Philip, Princess Margaret and their parents King George VI and Queen Elizabeth the Queen Mother attended the opening ceremony. Over fifty years later, Queen Elizabeth II and Prince Philip were back at the Royal Festival hall for the official re-opening ceremony following a major refurbishment of the facilities. The Royal Festival Hall has become one of the premier entertainment venues in London, with a constantly changing programme of concerts, music, dance, drama and performance. In 2018, Meghan Markle secretly attended Michelle Obama's talk entitled Becoming, before meeting Michelle Obama afterwards in a private audience.

Immediately adjacent to the Royal Festival Hall is another music venue – the Queen Elizabeth Hall, named in honour of the Queen. Just like the Royal Festival Hall, it is built in a Brutalist style with immense concrete sections. An unusual feature is the extensive concrete undercroft, popular with local

The Royal Festival Hall, Southbank has been the venue for numerous royal events.

skateboarders, performance artists, graffiti artists and BMXers.

The Duke and Duchess of Sussex attended the Nelson Mandela Centenary Exhibition here in 2018, when Meghan wore a pink mac dress created by the House of Nonie.

Nearest Underground

Waterloo 5 minutes
Embankment via the Golden Jubilee
   Bridge 8 minutes

www.southbankcentre.co.uk/venues/
royal-festival-hall

Shakespeare's Globe Theatre

21 New Globe Walk, Bankside, SE1 9DT

Shakespeare's Globe is unique in every way as it is a perfect reconstruction of the actual theatre used and part owned by William Shakespeare 400 years ago on this site. The original theatre burned down in 1613 when a props cannon used during a performance of Shakespeare's play *Henry VIII* misfired and set the wooden beams alight. In the late twentieth century, American actor/director Sam Wanamaker dreamed of recreating that theatre. His vision became reality in 1997 when Queen Elizabeth II and Prince Philip opened the newly reconstructed Globe Theatre.

A circular wooden structure, it is the first building in London constructed with a thatched roof since the 1666 Great Fire of London. Inside, spectators can sit in three tiers of seats, or just as in Shakespeare's time, stand in front of the

Opened by Queen Elizabeth, the Globe Theatre is an authentic recreation of William Shakespeare's Globe.

thrust-out stage. Plays are performed live, with no amplification, enabling audiences to experience what it would have been like 400 years ago.

Apart from attending plays, visitors can explore the theatre, adjacent exhibition centre and take part in guided tours explaining how the 'wooden O' works.

Tickets must be purchased for tours, performances and visits to the exhibition centre.

Opening hours
Exhibition 10am – 5pm
Theatre Tours 10.30am – 5pm

Nearest Underground
Blackfriars 10 minutes
Mansion House 10 minutes
Southwark 15 minutes

www.shakespearesglobe.com

Shard
Joiner Street, SE1 9QU

Dramatically positioned close to London Bridge, at 1,016ft (310m) tall the Shard is the tallest building in Western Europe. When visiting the Shard, Queen Elizabeth II accompanied by the Duke of Edinburgh, went onto the outdoor

The Shard is the tallest building in London, offering stunning views across the city.

viewing platform and asked to see a birds eye view of Buckingham Palace through the digital telescope. The views are definitely stunning. The viewing platforms are located on floors 68, 69 and 72 and provide 360° views for up to forty miles around the building. Don't worry about climbing stairs – high speed lifts take you from ground level to floor 68 in sixty seconds. The observation deck is in level 69, or you can head higher to level 72 with its open air sky deck. The Shard is covered in 11,000 glass panels – it takes seventeen window cleaners three months to clean the whole building.

Apart from viewing platform, the Shard also contains a hotel, restaurants and bars. Special events are often held here including silent discos and champagne parties. An unusual option once on the viewing platform is to book a virtual reality experience including the world's highest virtual slide!

Tickets must be pre-booked. All dated and timed for arrival, providing entry up to thirty minutes from the time printed on the ticket. Once on the viewing platforms, there are no time restrictions as how long you stay there.

Opening hours
10am – 10pm daily

Nearest Underground
London Bridge 1 minute

www.the-shard.com

Tate Modern
Bankside, SE1 9TG

Located in the iconic former Bankside power station, Tate Modern is a dramatic art museum. It focuses on British and international art, modern and contemporary, from 1900 to the present day. Much of the work is displayed in themed areas such as Artist and Society, Materials and Objects, and Living Cities. Notable exhibits include one of Yves Klein's Blue Panels, Dali's Lobster telephone, The Snail by Matisse and Picasso's Nude Woman with Necklace. There is a rotating programme of events and exhibitions.

Queen Elizabeth II officially opened The Tate Modern in 2000, during which she viewed the exhibits, and met artists and staff. Since its launch, the Tate has been extremely popular, attracting large numbers of people to its unique building. It is a massive art gallery, spanning several large buildings such as the Switch House with eleven floors. The Turbine House is a very large, open plan building and was highlighted on Princess Eugenie's Instagram account where the Princess recommended the Floating Fish exhibit. She is known to often post images of installations within the Turbine Hall.

Princess Eugenie is patron of the Tate Young Patrons organisation. This is a membership grouping described as being a 'sociable group with a contemporary focus, tailored for 18 – 40 year olds, exploring emerging artists and spaces.'

Princess Eugenie is closely linked to the Tate Modern art museum on Bankside.

Members receive invitations to VIP receptions, access to out of hours curator-led tours and numerous hosted events.

Entry free but exhibitions may incur a charge.

Nearest Underground
Bankside 9 minutes
Southwark 11 minutes

A dedicated high speed river ferry provides a fast connection between Tate Modern and Tate Britain, operating from Southwark Bankside Pier to Millbank Pier. Taking 17 minutes, it operates on an hourly basis.

www.tate.org.uk/visit/tate-modern

Thames Barrier

Unity Way, Woolwich, SE18 5NJ

The Thames Barrier has become one of the most instantly recognisable London sites. Stretching 520 metres across the river, this moveable barrier protects Greater London from flooding during high tides and North Sea storm surges. When raised, it is incredibly impressive as each gate stands 20 metres tall, weighs 3,300 tonnes and holds back 9,000 tonnes of water.

The system was officially opened in 1984 when Queen Elizabeth, accompanied by the Duke of Edinburgh, pressed a button to set the gates in motion. She had travelled down the river from Festival Pier to the Thames Barrier on board The Royal *Nore* barge.

Since then, the barrier has proved its value on many occasions. It has been raised as a defence 193 times between 1983 and May 2020. By far the greatest number of closures in one year was experienced in 2013 – 2014, when it prevented London from being flooded 50 times. The barrier has appeared in numerous film and TV shows, including the 2006 *Dr Who* Christmas Special and a *Top Gear* event in which presenter Jeremy Clarkson drove a racing boat through the barrier at high speed.

You can visit the Thames Barrier Information Centre to discover more about its construction and how it works. Check out the website to find out the monthly dates for scheduled closures of the barrier for maintenance and testing. Such closures are a unique opportunity to see the flood gates rotating into place. Each gate is hollow and is filled with water when submerged. The water slowly drains out as the gates emerge from the river.

The Thames Barrier is located between Greenwich and Silvertown, 1.9 miles east of the Isle of Dogs.

Opening times vary according to season
10.30am – 4.30pm daily in summer
11am – 3.30 pm Thursday to Sunday the
    rest of the year
Closed on bank holidays

Go to www.gov.uk/guidance/the-thames-barrier for a list of scheduled closures.

Thames River Cruises operate sight seeing cruises to Greenwich and the Barrier from Westminster Pier

Nearest Train
Charlton 19 minutes walk

www.visitlondon.com/things-to-do/place/26941-thames-barrier-information-centre

Wimbledon All England Lawn Tennis and Croquet Club

Church Road, Wimbledon, SW19 5AG

The Princess of Wales is patron of the All England Lawn Tennis Club, and frequently attends matches during the World Tennis Championships. She took over as patron of the club from Queen Elizabeth II in 2017, and is a huge supporter of the sport. The Princess of Wales always attends the Championships finals and awards the trophy to the winner.

Meghan, Duchess of Sussex, attended Wimbledon twice, once in Kate's company, and once on her own.

Book early for tickets for the Championships as there is tremendous demand. A limited number of tickets are available on the door each day of the Lawn Tennis Championships, but queues tend to be very long. All Centre Court tickets for the last four days of the tournament are always sold out in advance.

The Princess of Wales is patron of Wimbledon – an international arena familiar to all top players.

Exploring the history of tennis at the Wimbledon Lawn Tennis Museum (All England Lawn Tennis Club Lawn Tennis Museum).

Apart from the Championships, you can also visit the Wimbledon Lawn Tennis Museum all year round. This enables you to go behind the scenes and enjoy a ninety minute tour of the grounds and participate in a virtual reality experience showing how the event has grown and developed. Visitors are able to sit in the media centre, go through the players' doors, see the player facilities and discover how the perfect grass court is created.

Within the museum itself, you see the trophies and find out about the traditions and history of the game, as well as participating in hands-on activities testing tennis skills and feeling the fabric of tennis fashions.

Guided tours have to be prebooked.

Museum open
10am – 5pm daily

Nearest Underground
Southfields 15 minutes
Wimbledon Park Road 15 minutes
Wimbledon Station 23 minutes

www.wimbledon.com

EAST LONDON

Aladin

132 Brick Lane, Shadwell, E1 6RU

Ask the owners nicely and they will play back a recording of King Charles III praising the Aladin curry house. He had been on a visit to the Brick Lane area, and was interviewed on radio talking about his experiences. Apart from this royal accolade, Aladin has won a variety of awards, including the Taste Brick Lane Curry, European Curry and London Curry Awards.

Brick Lane is a centre of Indian cuisine, and Aladin has been described as one of the best in the area. It was originally opened in 1979 to cater for the local Bangladeshi community and its reputation has grown steadily. A small restaurant, space is limited inside but take-out is available. It offers Bangladeshi, Indian and Pakistani curries, baltis and grills.

Aladin is located close to the popular Brick Lane Sunday market as well as venues like the Truman Brewery.

Opening hours
Monday to Thursday 12 midday –
    12 midnight
Friday and Saturday 12 midday – 1am
Sunday 12 midday – 10.30pm

www.aladinbricklane.co.uk

Dennis Severs House

18 Folgate Street, Spitalfields, E1 6BX

This is possibly the most unusual, and most unexpected of all royal connections. Fascinated by history, Dennis Severs was an eccentric American intent on recreating the past. For many years, he conducted horse-drawn tours through the back streets of west London saying that 'the atmosphere of these backwaters – along with the clip-clop of the horse – worked as a time machine, and I was soon beginning to speak in the "dramatic present" as if things in the past where happening right now.'

The tours were extremely popular until one day when a developer purchased the stables and evicted both him and his horse. According to the *Daily Telegraph*, the Queen offered him a stable in the Royal Mews, where he stayed for some time and acquired his first cat, which he named Madge, short for Her Majesty. All his subsequent cats shared the same name.

Eventually moving on from the Royal Mews, he set about recreating the world of an eighteenth century Huguenot weaving family in Spitalfields, while actually living in the house and conducting atmospheric tours. Severs said that he set out to bring it back to life by sleeping in each of the rooms 'to arouse my intuition in the quest for each room's soul' so that 'the material things I had been collecting all my life were really a cast of characters, and the house was designed to be their stage.'

Following his death, Dennis Severs House has become an unusual atmospheric museum with rooms telling the story of its occupants from 1724 to 1914, creating a 'still life drama'. Visitors are encouraged to stay silent throughout the visit so as to experience the full atmosphere.

Tours begin at the cellar door, pass through the kitchen, dining room and smoking room, then end by passing through various bedrooms. Fires burn on the hearth, candles flicker, meals lie half eaten on the table, wigs hang over the backs of chairs and clocks tick and chime.

Entry charge.

Opening hours
Monday/Wednesday/Friday 5pm – 9pm
Sunday 12 midday – 3.15 pm

Nearest Underground
Liverpool Street 6 minutes
Aldgate East 11 minutes
Aldgate 11 minutes

www.dennissevershouse.co.uk

Queen Elizabeth Olympic Park
Stratford, E20 2ST

Who can forget that amazing opening scene at the 2012 London Olympic Games when Queen Elizabeth's double parachuted in, accompanied by James Bond, before attention switched to the Queen herself elsewhere in the arena. Queen Elizabeth had insisted on taking a speaking part in the parachuting

The ArcelorMittal Observation Tower in the Queen Elizabeth Olympic Park.

film, using the iconic words 'Good Evening, Mr Bond.' Queen Elizabeth also attended the closing ceremony while Prince William, Kate Middleton and Prince Harry were frequently seen attending events throughout the Games.

Following the Games, the site was renamed Queen Elizabeth Olympic Park, celebrating her Diamond Jubilee. The Park is now an active leisure complex covering many sporting activities such as cycling trials in the Velo park, as well as live music, theatre and arts in the Park. The Princess of Wales has visited on numerous occasions including playing volleyball in the Copper Box while wearing high wedge shoes, and scoring a goal with Team GB hockey players in the Riverbank area. In 2019, Meghan accompanied Prince Harry to attend a reception with former Invictus players and watch a baseball game at the stadium. In October 2022, the new Prince & Princess of Wales attended a reception and took part in activities to mark the 10th anniversary of the Coach Core scheme.

Dominating the site is the impressive ArcelorMittal Orbit Observation Tower. This was originally constructed as part of the Olympic Games complex, and was retained as a public monument afterwards. It is the largest public work of art in the UK. Visitors can climb to the top, view the skyline and see the world turned upside down using spectacular mirrors. In 2016, a massive 178 metre helter-skelter style slide was attached to the tower. This is now the world's longest and tallest slide of its kind worldwide. The 40 second trip from the top to bottom involves speeds of up to 15 miles per hour.

Entrance fee payable to the ArcelorMittal Orbit Tower.

Tower Opening hours
10am – 7pm daily

Nearest Underground
Stratford 13 minutes walk

www.queenelizabetholympicpark.co.uk

V&A Museum of Childhood
Bethnal Green

Discover your inner child at this fascinating museum, which is the largest of its kind in the world. Opened by the Prince of Wales (later Edward VII) in 1872 as a general museum containing various items from the Great Exhibition, it steadily became more child orientated. In the 1920s and 1930s Queen Mary (wife of King George V) donated many toys to the museum. It now contains a vast range of toys from the 1600s to the present day, including teddy bears, dolls houses, dolls, puppets, games, clothing, train sets, rocking horses and much more. It is very hands-on with lots of toys for children to play with, including dressing up areas. There is a regular programme of special events and exhibitions.

The Princess of Wales is patron of the museum. Staff were astounded when she arrived unexpectedly in 2012 on a private visit to discover the services it offers and take a look around.

Entry is free, but exhibitions may incur an extra charge.

Opening hours
10am – 5.45pm daily

Nearest Underground
Bethnal Green 1 minute

www.vam.ac.uk/moc

Violet Bakery

Wilton Way, Hackney, E8 3ED

A small bakery in Hackney, East London, it was relatively unknown until 2018 when Prince Harry and Meghan Markle announced that its owner was making their lemon and elderflower wedding cake. Violet Bakery is a Californian style bakery, owned by Claire Ptak, an American baker and food writer who focuses on using seasonal ingredients. On sale daily are a range of classic cakes, cup cakes, and buns as well as unusual ones such as chocolate-vanilla sandwich cookies and fruity spelt cake. Both sweet and savoury eat-in or takeaway options are available.

Opening hours
Monday to Friday 8am – 6pm
Weekends 9.30am – 6pm

Nearest Underground
Bethnal Green 30 minutes

www.violetcakes.com

GREENWICH

Greenwich is definitely spectacular. Its dramatic river frontage with its white buildings was created on the orders of Charles II, and it is now a UNESCO World Heritage site. Not only that, it is truly a royal area as Queen Elizabeth II granted royal borough status as part of her Diamond Jubilee celebrations. For hundreds of years, it had one of the favourite royal palaces, and the birthplace of the Tudor Queen Elizabeth I in 1533.

Cutty Sark

Lower ground, The Dock, SE10 9HT

Once the fastest ship in the world, the *Cutty Sark* has been opened by Queen Elizabeth II twice, in 1957 and then again following restoration in 2012. This is a magnificent sleek vessel and is unique. The Cutty Sark is the world's only surviving Tea Clipper, now over 150 years old. It was built with one aim in mind, to bring tea back from the Far East as quickly as possible. Eventually it carried many other cargoes, including wool, covering vast distances as a working cargo vessel, and later as a training ship. It has been calculated that the *Cutty Sark* travelled the

equivalent of two and a half voyages to the moon and bank.

Visitors can stand under the ship and see what would have been under the sea when travelling the oceans, while discovering how it was constructed. On board, you can hold the wheel, learn how to steer, explore the Captain's Cabin, climb into bunk beds, and find out what life would have been like for sailors crewing this stunning ship. The Cutty Sark is also home to the biggest collection of carved wooden figureheads which used to decorate ships' prows.

Entry is by ticket only.

Opening hours
10am – 5pm daily

Nearest DLR
Greenwich Pier 6 minutes

Nearest Train
Greenwich 10 minutes

www.rmg.co.uk/cutty-sark

Greenwich Park

SE10 8HQ

The vast green lawns of this beautiful park once formed a hunting area for Tudor Kings and Queens. They enjoyed strolling in the park and relaxing with a meal. Check out the massive tree known as Queen Elizabeth's Oak, estimated to have been planted in the twelfth century. According to stories, Queen Elizabeth I once picnicked under its shady branches.

Greenwich Park has now become the location for a much bigger event of royal interest – the London Marathon. Every year, thousands of runners begin this marathon from the lofty heights of Greenwich Park. Prince Harry was patron of the London Marathon Charitable Trust. One royal who has successfully taken part in the London Marathon was Princess Beatrice in 2010. She took five hours, thirteen minutes and four seconds to complete the run. In 2018, Queen Elizabeth II started the London Marathon via a satellite link from Windsor Castle. She stepped onto a podium in front of the Round Tower and pressed the start button at 10.00 am to set off 40,000 runners along the 26-mile course.

This is definitely a fantastic place to relax – quite apart from the pleasures of the green lawns and deer park, you can stroll through rose, herb and flower gardens, admire the largest herbaceous border in London and inspect the fruit in the Queen's Orchard or enjoy the iconic views of the Thames.

Free to enter.

Opening hours
6am daily
Closing time varies seasonally between
6pm – 9.30pm

Nearest DLR and boat pier
Greenwich Pier 6 minutes

Nearest Train
Greenwich 10 minutes

www.royalparks.org.uk/parks/greenwich-park

National Maritime Museum

Romney Road, Greenwich, SE10 9NF

As a former Royal Navy officer, it was very apt that Prince Philip was patron of the National Maritime Museum. The Prince Philip Maritime Collection within the museum is named in his honour. In 2011, he opened the new Sammy Ofer wing containing a special exhibitions gallery, library and a new permanent gallery called Voyagers, looking at the story of Britain and the sea.

Queen Elizabeth II had a long history of involvement with the Museum. She attended the Museum's official opening back in 1937. Her father, King George VI, performed the opening ceremony accompanied by his wife, Queen Elizabeth the Queen Mother, and the young eleven-year-old Princess Elizabeth.

Strolling round the Museum you can discover maritime history in all its forms – from Pacific Encounters to stories of exploration and exploitation, the real Pirates of the Caribbean, climate change within Polar regions, the Tudor and Stuart seafarers who created history, such as Sir Francis Drake's circumnavigation of the world and his welcome home by Queen Elizabeth I, to war and nature. See a royal barge built for an eighteenth century Prince of Wales, stand beside one of the most photographed art works in London in the form of a replica HMS *Victory* in a bottle, and admire the coat worn by Admiral Nelson during the Battle of Trafalgar. Other unusual objects include a nineteenth century Polar oversuit and Captain Scott's shoes.

Free entry, but special exhibitions may incur a charge.

Opening hours
10am – 5pm daily

Nearest DLR
Greenwich Pier 6 minutes

Nearest Train
Greenwich 10 minutes
Boat from Tower Pier to Greenwich Pier
　6 minutes

www.rmg.co.uk

O2 Arena

Peninsula Square, SE10 0DX

A spectacular dome-shaped building on the edge of Greenwich, The O2 Arena began life as the Millennium Dome. It was designed as the centrepiece of the UK's millennium celebrations and was opened by Queen Elizabeth II. She arrived by boat on 31 December 1999 and the resultant event became known as one of the biggest PR disasters in history. Thousands of VIPs missed the actual ceremony or arrived late due to traffic problems and extensive security checks. Queen Elizabeth was seen holding hands with the Prime Minster, Tony Blair, during a massive rendition of *Auld Lang Syne* as the new century arrived.

Over the next twelve months, the lack of public interest in the displays within the Dome led to it being dubbed a 'white elephant'. It was eventually closed, sold and then rebranded the O2 Arena. In 2007, the O2 Arena opened as a sports, entertainment and leisure complex with Bon Jovi as the first musician to perform on site. Since then many famous names have been involved, including the Rolling Stones, Beyoncé, One Direction and two of the greatest names in opera – Placido Domingo and Angela Gheorghiu. In 2012, it was used as a London Olympic venue hosting gymnastic displays and the basketball finals.

The O2 Arena is now one of the most popular entertainment venues in the country, able to cater for 20,000 spectators under its dome, which measures 365 metres in diameter. The site also includes exhibition areas, a music club, cinema, piazzas, bars, restaurants and an ICON shopping

The O2 Arena seen from above, with the River Thames and Canary Wharf in the background.

outlet where you can buy premium brands at discount prices.

One of the most popular attractions at the O2 does require a head for heights, as you can book a climb over the exterior of the massive dome. There are specific time slots available for this experience, which must be pre-booked. A glass stairway leads to the start of the 380 metre long fabric walkway. Before starting the climb it is necessary to don climbing gear, including a harness for safety.

A guide takes small groups up the walkway, allowing time at different points to admire the view. There is a 30 degree incline at the steepest point, before reaching the 52 metre high summit. Once on the top viewing platform, harnesses are unclipped allowing participants to walk around for about 20 minutes to enjoy the stunning views.

Tours and performances incur a charge.

Opening hours
9am – 1am daily

Nearest Underground
North Greenwich 2 minutes
By boat from Embankment Pier to
    North Greenwich Pier

www.theo2.co.uk

Old Royal Naval College

Greenwich, SE10 9NN

Royalty has been coming to this site for centuries. Underneath the pristine lawns and beautiful buildings we see today, lie the remains of a Tudor palace, a favourite home for Henry VIII and all his six wives, as well as Elizabeth I and her sister Queen Mary I. Henry VIII married two of his wives here, Catherine of Aragon and Anne of Cleves. Elizabeth I was particularly fond of Greenwich; it was her birthplace and childhood home, and when Queen she spent many summers at the palace. Some parts of that Tudor palace can be seen on display in the Undercroft of the Old Royal Naval College – who knows, perhaps they were once used by those legendary royals!

The Chapel is built on the site of the original royal chapel, and includes an altarpiece by artist Benjamin West. Princess Anne, The Princess Royal came to celebrate the completion of the Painted Hall conservation project. She enjoyed a Gala dinner amid the splendour of the Painted Hall as well as watching a Beating the Retreat performance by the Royal Marines Band and the Corps of Drums.

The Painted Hall is often described as Britain's Sistine Chapel – and it is easy to see why. It took Sir James Thornhill nineteen years to paint this dramatic ceiling, which neatly complements the Baroque architecture of Sir Christopher Wren. Look closely at the paintings and you can find some instantly recognisable London sites hidden away such as images of St Paul's Cathedral.

A Canaletto-style view of the Old Royal Naval College on the River Thames.

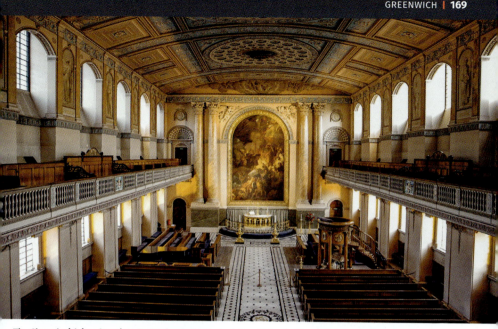

The Chapel with its altarpiece by Benjamin West, depicting St Paul shipwrecked on the island of Malta.

Stand on the promenade by the river and admire the stunning location – a UNESCO World Heritage site, it has a distinct resemblance to a Canaletto painting. By the seventeenth century, the Tudor palace had fallen into disuse, and Charles II decided to give it another purpose. He asked Sir Christopher Wren to build a Royal Hospital for Seamen on the site, which later became a Royal Naval College providing officer training. As you stroll around the buildings and grounds some of the scenes may look rather familiar – which is not surprising as it is a popular film and TV location. Remember the grand vistas of 'Paris' and the funeral procession of Lamarque in *Les Miserables*, or Robert Downey's/ Guy Ritchie's version of *Sherlock Holmes*

with rioting outside the Houses of Parliament or Grand Hotel shots? Look no further than the Old Royal Naval College. Other films shot here include *Pirates of the Caribbean On Stranger Tides*, *The Kings Speech* and *Skyfall*. It also provided the perfect location for scenes showing the courtyard entrance of Buckingham Palace in *The Crown*, with Matt Smith (the Duke of Edinburgh) seen among the distinctive white pillars.

Entry to the Painted Hall is by ticket, and this includes access to the Victorian Skittle Alley where you can try your hand at getting a strike.

Guided tours are often available throughout the day, including tours of film and TV locations. These are free to Painted Hall ticket holders.

The magnificently restored eighteenth-century Painted Hall by James Thornhill.

Opening hours
10am – 5pm daily

Nearest DLR station
Greenwich Pier 6 minutes

Nearest Train
Greenwich 10 minutes
By boat from Tower Pier
Greenwich Pier 6 minutes

www.ornc.org

Queen's House

Romney Road, SE10 9NF

Part of the National Maritime Museum, this is one of the most elegant art galleries in London. The first classical building in England, the royal family used it until 1805. After that it became a home for the orphans of seamen, before being turned into an art gallery. On display are some of the most impressive masterpieces, such as the incredibly detailed Armada portrait of Elizabeth I placed within the Queen's Presence Chamber, plus works by Turner and Canaletto. Even the ceiling in the Queen's Presence Chamber is superbly painted, reflecting the fact that this was once the bedroom of the doomed King Charles I's wife, Queen Henrietta Maria. Not to be missed is the amazing Tulip self supporting spiral staircase and the delicate gold leaf fresco ornamenting the Great Hall ceiling.

Opening hours
10am – 5pm daily

Nearest DLR
Greenwich Pier 6 minutes

Nearest Train
Greenwich 10 minutes
Boat from Embankment or Tower Pier
    to Greenwich Pier

www.rmg.co.uk/queens-house

Royal Observatory

Blackheath Avenue, SE10 8XJ

Become a time lord and stand on time at the Royal Observatory. Founded by Charles II, it is from this spot that every location on earth is measured. This is where east truly meets west at Longitude 0 degrees. Stand with one foot on either side of the line, and you are perfectly in the middle of the world as well as time, since the prime meridian also acts as the reference point for time worldwide. All time everywhere is measured exactly from this point. Look out for the bright red time ball on top of Flamsteed House. An early public time signal, the ball rises half way up the mast at 12.55; at 12.58 it moves to the top; and at 1pm exactly it drops, providing an exact marker for Greenwich mean time.

While at the Royal Observatory take the opportunity to travel into space via a Planetarium show, see clocks and timepieces that have changed the way the world has operated, discover historic telescopes and stories of dramatic discoveries, and visit Flamsteed House where the Astronomers Royal lived and worked. Stop off in the Camera Obscura for a very surprising view of Greenwich.

Tickets required – you can get joint tickets combining entry to the *Cutty Sark*.

Opening hours
10am – 5pm daily

Nearest DLR
Greenwich Pier 6 minutes

Nearest Train
Greenwich 10 minutes

www.rmg.co.uk/royal-observatory